SONG AND DANCE
ACTIVITIES
FOR
ELEMENTARY
CHILDREN

Also by the Author

Music Today and Every Day, Parker Publishing Company, Inc., 1979.

SONG AND DANCE ACTIVITIES FOR ELEMENTARY CHILDREN

Harriet R. Reeves

Illustrations by Kate Gartner

Parker Publishing Company, Inc.
West Nyack, New York

10 9 8 7 6 5 4

Library of Congress Cataloging-in-Publication Data

Reeves, Harriet
  Song and dance activities for elementary children.

  Includes index.
  1. Educational games.   2. Singing games—Study and
teaching (Elementary)   3. Games with music—Study and
teaching (Elementary)   I. Title.
LB1029.G3R44   1985   372.13'078   85-12029

ISBN 0-13-822677-6

About the Author

Harriet Ramsey Reeves is a Professor of Education at the University of Miami in Coral Gables, Florida, where she teaches music fundamentals and music materials and methods to elementary education majors. A veteran elementary and junior high school music teacher, Dr. Reeves holds a Bachelor of Music Education degree and both an M.S. and an Ed.D. in elementary education.

She has published another book on music, *Music Today and Every Day*, also published by Parker Publishing Company, Inc., and several articles that appeared in *The Music Educator's Journal, The Instructor, Language Arts*, and *The Reading Teacher*. Dr. Reeves' special area of interest is the teaching of academic skills through music, and this has been the subject of many of her workshops. This book is an outgrowth of her conviction that music is for everyone and that it can enhance the quality of life, regardless of one's skill level in music.

About This Book

Song and Dance Activities for Elementary Children is a collection of finger plays, action songs, singing games, folk dances, and other musical activities that involve the participation of all children of ages four to thirteen. Included in this book is everything from perennial favorites that have been used for many years, to songs and activities that may not be so well-known. Thus, it can serve as a source book for elementary teachers to use to locate and review fondly remembered musical activities or to find new ones for a variety of purposes.

The song and dance games presented here are those that have proven popular with children of all ages, along with some lesser known ones that should become favorites as the children learn them and participate in them. They are appropriate for school activities directed by elementary and nursery classroom and music teachers, for recreation and camp programs, for church-sponsored activities, and for other young people's organizations, such as the scouts and 4-H Clubs. Generally, no special music skills are required of the leader or director of the activities in this book and many of them involve songs or tunes that are well-known to children.

The book is divided into three major parts: "Action Songs and Activities," "Singing Activities and Games for One or More Students," and, "Dance Games and Activities for Large Groups." The activities, dances, and games have been divided according to the size of the area required to do them and the number of students who need to move from their desks to the open space. The activities in each part are arranged in order of difficulty.

Part One, "Action Songs and Activities," contains songs and activities that may be performed without requiring students to move away from their desks. Many action songs and finger plays, as well as games, are included. In some cases, students can remain in their seats; in others, they may need to stand beside their desks. Generally, they require a minimum of time to perform, since the students' movement is restricted. The range of difficulty is from very easy, including some suitable for preschool and primary children, to more difficult, which are suitable for upper elementary students and older children.

The activities in Part Two, "Singing Activities and Games for One or More Students," require some open space area, the size depending on the individual activity and the number of students. The dramatization of songs and games requiring one or a few students to perform are included in this section. As one or more students must move away from their desks and the performers may change in the starring roles when the games or activities are repeated, a larger block of time may be desirable.

Again, the games and activities represent a wide range of difficulty, from very easy to more difficult. Those using the book should remember that the degree of difficulty is not always a reliable guide for the grade placement of the activities, as older children often enjoy doing some of the easier activities. Subject matter appeal and sufficient physical coordination are important considerations in deciding on appropriate grade placement.

Part Three, "Dance Games and Activities for Large Groups," contains activities requiring large, open areas, the size depending upon the group size. The smallest effective group size for activities in this part is five to eight students. The maximum size is limited by open space and means of amplifying sound. Partners may be used in some of the dances, though in most cases they are not necessary. Methods of overcoming problems associated with dances requiring partners are discussed in the introduction to Part Three.

More time will usually be required for the dances and activities than those in Parts One and Two, as there is student movement away from their desks into special formations, and directions must be given more precisely and carefully. If the activity is being introduced for the first time, demonstrations with smaller groups should be given before the entire group participates. This also takes more time.

As in the other sections, there are dances and games appropriate for all ages in the elementary school. Teachers and leaders may select activities of varying difficulty, based on the group's prior experience, their maturity level, and the amount of time available to teach and perform the activity. For example, a relatively simple dance or game may be selected for a fifth grade class if the teacher wants a satisfactory performance in a short period of time. Prime consideration should be given to the appropriateness of the subject matter, as fifth graders would be insulted if asked to perform "The Farmer in the Dell," but not the "Hokey Pokey," even though the latter is often done by primary age children.

Each activity is presented in the format of a lesson plan, complete with objectives and step-by-step procedures, to minimize the amount of preparation necessary for anyone wishing to use them. Each activity begins with a short summary or description listed below the title for anyone who needs to make a selection quickly and does not have time to scan through the entire page of directions. These time-saving aids are provided because of the many demands already made of the book's users. For this reason, the entire book is designed as a "quick" reference, organized in an easily understood format.

These dances, games, and activities can serve a multitude of purposes, including entertainment and amusement, movement activities for those who need a change of pace, development of body rhythm, and practice in sequencing, following directions, and other academic skills. As you use *Song and Dance Activities for Elementary Children*, you will begin to realize that it is indeed a treasury filled with interesting, challenging, and spicy musical activities to enliven any gathering of children. It can make the difference between an ordinary or an exciting, enjoyable environment. It's all here, waiting for you to make the contents come alive!

Harriet R. Reeves

Contents

II SINGING ACTIVITIES AND GAMES FOR ONE OR MORE STUDENTS • 67

III DANCE GAMES AND ACTIVITIES
FOR LARGE GROUPS • 145

SONG AND DANCE
ACTIVITIES
FOR
ELEMENTARY
CHILDREN

I

ACTION SONGS
AND ACTIVITIES

Part I consists of musical activities that can be performed in a limited amount of space and time. This is possible because no special formations are required. All of the songs and activities can be performed while students are seated or stand beside their desks. In some cases there should be enough room to bend, turn around, and so on, without bumping into objects or their neighbors. Some activities that can be performed while sitting or standing are: "Open, Shut Them," "Where Is Thumbkin?," "Cabin in the Wood," "Bingo," "Jimmy Crack Corn," and "Guess the Pattern." Activities that require standing with sufficient space to move and bend are: "I Know a Little Pussy," "Head, Shoulders, Knees and Toes," "One Finger, One Thumb," "Abe Lincoln Had Many Sons," and "Busy Song." Still other activities lend themselves to a standing position but require very little additional space, such as "We're in, Right Out," "I'm a Little Teapot," "Angel Band," and "The Noble Duke of York."

Some of the variations suggested with certain activities may or may not be suitable for performance in the limited space and time constraints imposed by this section. For instance, if variation 1 suggested for "Angel Band" were performed, ten children would need to come to a limited open-space area at the front of the room for the special activity.

Almost anyone—even those without special music skills—can direct groups in the action songs and activities listed. If children untrained in music can perform them, then so can adults with minimal music skills. In addition, many of the songs used are familiar to citizens of the United States, thus minimizing the need for musical skills to learn new songs.

Action songs and activities range from easy to difficult for children of elementary age, indicating that some of them may also be appropriate for younger and older children. Even though some songs and activities may be easy to perform, they are fun for children in a wide range of ages. For instance, songs such as "If You're Happy and You Know It" and "Head, Shoulders, Knees and Toes" may appeal to all elementary children even though they are not particularly difficult. Other songs and activities, such as "Teddy Bear," "I'm a Little Teapot," and "Busy Song," may be appropriate and appealing only for children through grades two or three. On the other hand, songs and activities such as "Stodola Pumpa" and "An Austrian Went Yodeling" require more physical coordination and sequencing skills and are more suitable for older elementary children.

I–1   OPEN, SHUT THEM   Grades K–2

A simple finger play that follows the words of the song.

Objective: To move the fingers and hands rhythmically while singing.

Formation: An individual activity that may be done seated or standing by the desk.

Open, Shut Them

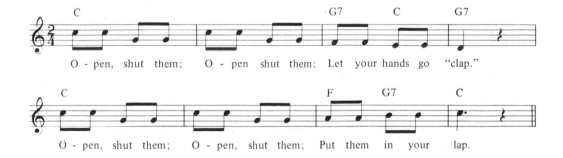

Verse 2:

Walk them, walk them, walk them, walk them,
Right up to your chin.
Open up your little mouth,
But do not walk them in.

Procedure:

1. Introduce this song as a movement song for the hands and fingers. Mention that the words tell what to do.

2. Teach the song and movements as follows:

Open, shut them; open shut them; Hold hands in front about chest high with palms facing away from the body. Open and close the fingers as indicated by the words. (Watch to see that children do not close the fingers as they sing *open* and vice-versa.)

Let your hands go "clap." Clap your hands once on the word *"clap."*

Open, shut them, Open, shut them; Open and close fingers as indicated by the words.

Put them in your lap. Put the back of one hand into the palm of the other one and place them in your lap.

Walk them, walk them, walk them, walk them; "Walk" the first and second fingers on the right hand on the left arm, starting at the wrist and going up to the shoulder.

Right up to your chin. Continue to walk the fingers past the left shoulder to the chin, and pause.

Open up your little mouth, Hold the prior position.

But do not walk them in. Remove the right fingers from the left shoulder and move the index finger and head from side to side as if to say, "No."

3. After children know the song and the motions fairly well, invite one or more to come to the front to lead it.

I–2   WHERE IS THUMBKIN?   Grades K–2

A finger play featuring a different finger in each verse.

Objectives: To do rhythmic motions following the words of the song. To change the last verse dealing with all the fingers from singular verbs, nouns, and pronouns to plural ones.

Formation: An individual activity that may be done sitting or, preferably, standing beside the desk.

Where Is Thumbkin?

Where is Thumb-kin? Where is Thumb-kin? Here I am. Here I am.

How are you to-day, sir? Ver-y well, I thank you. Run a-way. Run a-way.

Procedure:

1. Teach the first verse with motions as follows:

   Where is Thumbkin? Where is Thumbkin? Both hands are behind the back.

   Here I am. Here I am. On the first "Here I am." bring the left hand to the front with the thumb extended upward. The fingers should be closed. On the second "Here I am." bring the right hand to the front with the thumb extended upward.

   How are you today, sir? Move the left thumb rhythmically, as though talking to the other thumb.

   Very well, I thank you, Move the right thumb rhythmically, as though responding to the left thumb.

   Run away. Run away. On the first "Run away." put the left hand behind the back, and on the second one, put the right hand behind the back.

2. The words and motions for the next five verses are very similar to verse one, except that a different finger or fingers are used. The verses are as follows:

   Where is pointer? (First finger)
   Where is tall man? (Tallest or second finger)
   Where is ring man?
   Where is pinky?
   Where are all the men? Where are all the men?
   Here we are. Here we are.
   How are you today, sirs? Very well, we thank you.
   Run away. Run away.

3. After the song is learned well, student leaders can be used.

Variations:

1. Divide the group in half and appoint a student leader for each half. They sing the indicated parts:

   First half: *Where is thumbkin? Where is thumbkin?*

   Second half: *Here I am. Here I am.*

   First half: *How are you today, sir?*

   Second half: *Very well, I thank you.*

   Everyone: *Run away. Run away.*

2. Substitute individual students' names for thumbkin, so that this activity becomes a question-response interaction between the teacher or student group and the named individual. For instance, instead of singing *Where is thumbkin?* the teacher or class (the name will have to be decided in advance if the group is used) will substitute a student's name; for example, *Where is Mary? Where is Mary?* Mary would respond with a solo on the lines, *Here I am. Here I am.*

   Teacher/Group: *Where is Mary? Where is Mary?*

   Mary: *Here I am. Here I am.*

   Teacher/Group: *How are you today, M'am?*

   Mary: *Very well, I thank you.*

   Everyone: *Run away. Run away.*

I–3   THREE TIMES AROUND WENT THE GALLANT SHIP   Grades K–2

Objective: To move rhythmically according to the words of the song.

Formation: Individual actions with students standing in front of or by their desks.

Three Times Around Went the Gallant Ship

Procedure:

1. Teach children the song.
2. Do the following motions with the song after it is learned:

   Turn around once on each of the first three phrases (Phrase 1: *Three times around went the gallant ship;* phrase 2: *And three times around went she;* phrase 3: *And three times around went the gallant ship*), pausing slightly after each turn so that each of the three turns begins on the first beat of each phrase.

   On the last phrase, *And she sank to the bottom of the sea,* students should jump up and clap both hands together over their heads and gradually sink to the floor to emulate the sinking of the ship.

Variation:

If you wish, you can conduct this song as a singing game, in which case the students should form a circle. They join hands and do sliding steps to the side for the first three phrases. On the last phrase, they drop hands, jump up and clap both hands over their heads, and gradually sink to the floor.

I-4   BUSY SONG   Grades K-2

An action song that involves stepping, tapping, and clapping up high and down low.

Objectives: To move rhythmically to the words of the song. To develop the concepts of high and low.

Formation: An individual activity, that can be done standing beside the desk.

Busy Song

Alice E. Workman

We step, step, step, and tap, tap, tap, and then we turn a - round. We

step, step, step, and tap, tap, tap, and bow with - out a sound. We

clap down low, we clap up high. We clap the ground, we clap the sky. We

step, step, step, and tap, tap, tap, and then we sit right down.

From *Making Music Your Own*, Kindergarten, © 1971 Silver Burdett Company. Reprinted by permission.

Procedure:

1. Sing the song with actions:

   We step, step, step, Step three times with alternate feet.

   And tap, tap, tap, Tap three times with the same toe.

   And then we turn around. Turn around in place.

   We step, step, step, Step three times with alternate feet.

   And tap, tap, tap, Tap three times with the same toe.

And bow without a sound. Girls curtsy and boys bow.

We clap down low, Bend down with hands in front and clap three times on the words "clap down low."

We clap up high. Stand up straight and lift hands above the head and clap three times on the words "clap up high."

We clap the ground, Bend down with hands in front and clap three times on the words "clap the ground,"

We clap the sky. Stand up straight and lift hands above the head and clap three times on the words "clap the sky."

We step, step, step, Step three times with alternate feet.

And tap, tap, tap, Tap three times with the same toe.

And then we sit right down. Everyone sits down in his seat.

2. On the second and third times through the song, invite students to do the motions with you and to try singing the words if they wish.

3. To teach the words by rote, the song may need to be divided into several parts, with the teacher singing one part and the students repeating it. This procedure is followed for each part of the song, and then everyone sings the entire song all the way through (without stopping, unless a portion needs more work).

Variation:

Children may compose new words and actions to the song, such as *We run, run, run, and hop, hop, hop, and stoop down to the ground.*

I–5   THE PEOPLE ON THE BUS   Grades K–3

An action song in which children do motions that are appropriate to the words of the song.

Objectives: To move rhythmically while emulating various activities associated with riding a bus. To acquaint children with the various aspects of riding a bus.

Formation: An individual activity, which can be done standing beside the desk.

The People on the Bus

Verse 2:

The wheels on the bus go round and round.

Verse 3:

The horn on the bus goes beep, beep, beep.

Verse 4:

The money in the box goes ding, ding, ding.

Verse 5:

The wipers on the bus go swish, swish, swish.

Verse 6:

The driver on the bus says, "Move on back."

Verse 7:

The baby on the bus goes, "Wah, wah, wah."

Procedure:

1. Teach the first verse to the children and let them suggest an appropriate movement.
2. Sing the other verses after children decide on the movements. Select a different child for each verse to be the leader who decides on the motion.

Variations:

1. Instead of teaching all the verses above, teach only one or two verses and invite the children to compose additional ones.

2. Dramatize the song by appointing four children to be the wheels, one child to be the bus driver, two children to be the windshield wipers, one child to be the horn, one child to be the baby, one child to be the customer putting money in the box, and several children to be riders or people on the bus. The children should station themselves according to the part they are playing so that a bus is suggested. Only the role players will do the suggested motions and sing the action words. For instance, on the first verse, only those students playing the part of the people on the bus will go up and down and sing those words; only the four students playing the role of the wheels will make a motion indicating the turning of the wheels and will sing the words "round and round."

I–6   EENCY WEENCY SPIDER   Grades K–3

A finger play done by children at their desks.

Objective: To move rhythmically, interpreting the words of the song.

Formation: An individual activity, which can be done seated or standing beside the desk.

Eency Weency Spider

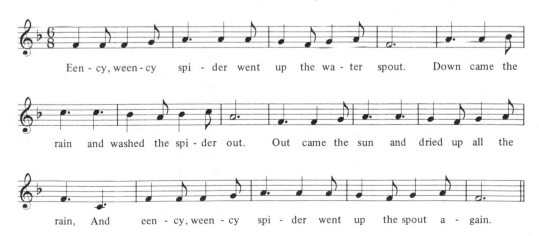

Een - cy, ween - cy spi - der went up the wa - ter spout. Down came the
rain and washed the spi - der out. Out came the sun and dried up all the
rain, And een - cy, ween - cy spi - der went up the spout a - gain.

Procedure:

1. Teach the above song and motions simultaneously.

   Eeency, weency spider went up the water spout.

   With the left arm bent at the elbow so that the hand and lower arm are in a vertical position, the first and second fingers of the right hand walk up the vertical part of the left arm.

   Down came the rain and washed the spider out.

   Extend both hands above the head and gradually lower them to waist level, moving fingers rhythmically to emulate the falling of rain.

   Out came the sun and dried up all the rain,

   Again, extend both hands above the head, forming a circle with the fingers by touching the two thumbs and the two second fingers. Gradually bring hands down in a wide circular motion to represent the beaming downward of the sun's rays. This downward movement continues until hands are about waist level, ready for the next movement.

   And eency, weency spider went up the spout again.

   Do the same movement as for the first phrase.

Variations:

1. An alternate movement for the first and fourth phrases that requires more muscular coordination, and, consequently, may be more appropriate for older children, is:

   Alternatively touch the second finger of one hand with the thumb of the other hand to represent the climbing of the spider; the second finger of the left hand touches the thumb of the right hand; twist the hands in a semicircle, with the touching finger and thumb as a pivotal point, so that the second finger of the right hand touches the thumb of the left hand (as soon as the "new" finger and thumb touch, release the contact of the "old" finger and thumb); twist the hands in a semicircle in the opposite direction, with the touching finger and thumb as a pivotal point, until the second finger and thumb of opposite hands touch; at this point, release the contact between the other finger and thumb. This continues throughout the first and fourth phrases.

2. Instead of using hand motions for the song, rhythm instruments may be used in this manner:

Phrase 1: One or more students play the tone blocks, sticks, or claves on the beat.

Phrase 2: One or more students play the tambourines, maracas, or jingle sticks, shaking them in a tremolo effect until the word "washed" at which time the instrument is hit firmly on the heel of the opposite hand.

Phrase 3: One or more students play the triangle, or finger cymbals on the beat.

Phrase 4: One or more students play the tone blocks, sticks, or claves on the beat.

I–7   I'M A LITTLE TEAPOT   Grades K–2

A simple action song for young children.

Objective: To move rhythmically while singing the song.

Formation: An individual activity, that can be done standing in front of or beside the desk.

I'm a Little Teapot

Words and Music by
C. Kelley and G. Sanders

Procedure:

1. Teach the song and motions simultaneously. The motions are:

   I'm a little teapot Place hands on hips.

   short and stout, Hands are held in a horizontal position with palms facing each other in front of the chest to indicate "short"; hands are then held in a side or vertical position with palms facing each other to indicate wideness or stoutness.

   Here is my handle, Place one hand on the hip.

   Here is my spout. Make a spout by placing the other arm to the side, bending the elbow so that the upper arm points upward; bend the hand at the wrist so that the open hand (palm facing downward) is in a downward position.

   When I get all steamed up then I shout, Hold the above position with hand on the hip and the other in a "spout" position.

   Just tip me over, pour me out. Bend over to the side as though pouring from the spout.

I-8   THE SEASONS   Grades K-3

   For each pair of verses concerning a season, a different child is chosen to come to the front of the class to state the activity he wishes for that season and to demonstrate an appropriate movement, which is to be imitated by the other class members.

Objective: To interpret the words of the song through creative movement.

Formation: One child comes to the front of the class to demonstrate and lead a movement for each unit of two verses. The remainder of the class stand by their desks and join in the demonstrated movement on the second verse.

The Seasons

1. Here's what we do in the win - ter - time, win - ter - time, win - ter - time.

Here's what we do in the win - ter - time when it's ver - y, ver - y cold.

Verse 2:

We ride our sleds in the wintertime, wintertime, wintertime.
We ride our sleds in the wintertime when it's very, very cold.

Verse 3:

Here's what we do in the springtime, springtime, springtime.
Here's what we do in the springtime when it's very, very warm.

Verse 4:

We sow the seeds in the springtime, springtime, springtime.
We sow the seeds in the springtime when it's very, very warm.

Verse 5:

Here's what we do in the summertime, summertime, summertime.
Here's what we do in the summertime when it's very, very hot.

Verse 6:

We like to swim in the summertime, summertime, summertime.
We like to swim in the summertime when it's very, very hot.

Verse 7:

Here's what we do in the autumntime, autumntime, autumntime.
Here's what we do in the autumntime when it's very, very cool.

Verse 8:

We rake the leaves in the autumntime, autumntime, autumntime.
We rake the leaves in the autumntime when it's very, very cool.

Procedure:

1. Teach the above song to the children, using a minimum of two verses. All may be done at this point if desired.

2. Demonstrate an action on the first verse and ask the class to join in the same action on the second verse.

3. Invite a student to demonstrate an action that would be appropriate for verses three and four. Have the student demonstrate on verse three and the entire class join in on verse four.

4. Call on another student to demonstrate an action that is appropriate for verses five and six. As above, the student demonstrates on verse five and the others join in on verse six.

5. Call on another student to lead in an appropriate action for verses seven and eight.

Variation:

Invite students to create their own verses and actions for each season. For instance, a student may be called on to make up a verse and lead the students. The class sings the first verse *Here's what we do in the wintertime.* They then wait for the leader to tell them the activity and show the motion (the new words should fit the tune), which might be, *We skate on ice in the wintertime* and he would do a skating movement. After he briefly shares this, they all join in singing and moving. Before moving on to the next season, several students could create a verse and related motion for winter.

The third verse, *Here's what we do in the springtime*, would then be sung. A student would be selected to create an activity and motion for the entire class to join in while singing the created fourth verse. Before moving on to verse five, several others might be asked to create a verse and related motion for springtime. The other two seasons should be handled in much the same manner if there is time.

I-9   IF YOU'RE HAPPY AND YOU KNOW IT,
CLAP YOUR HANDS   Grades K-4

Motion words and related motions can be changed depending upon the desires of the children. Generally, the last verse contains an accumulation of all previous motions in sequence.

Objectives: To move rhythmically with the music. To remember and do a series of motions in sequence.

Formation: No special formation is required in this song. Children may stand or sit, depending upon the motions included and the wishes of the teacher or group.

If You're Happy and You Know It

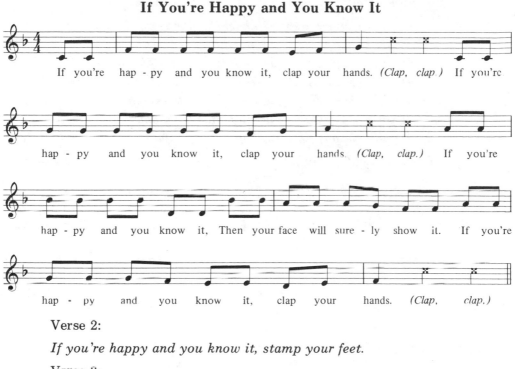

If you're hap-py and you know it, clap your hands. *(Clap, clap.)* If you're
hap-py and you know it, clap your hands. *(Clap, clap.)* If you're
hap-py and you know it, Then your face will sure-ly show it. If you're
hap-py and you know it, clap your hands. *(Clap, clap.)*

Verse 2:

If you're happy and you know it, stamp your feet.

Verse 3:

If you're happy and you know it, snap your fingers.

Verse 4:

If you're happy and you know it, do all three.
(clap clap, stamp, stamp, snap, snap)

Procedure:

1. Teach or review the above song, singing as many verses as you wish.

2. Sing the song with the indicated motions, making sure the claps, stamps, or snaps are done rhythmically. Usually, it is a good idea if you or a student who has good rhythm leads the motions. The last verse, which contains an accumulation of all the preceding motions, might need to be rehearsed slowly at first, but always rhythmically. After children feel comfortable with it, speed it up, even faster than the prior three verses, to challenge the children.

Variation:

Other motion words can be substituted in the song. It is also possible to include more than three verses. Other motions that might be used are:

If you're happy and you know it, shake your finger.
If you're happy and you know it, nod your head.
If you're happy and you know it, stoop right down.
If you're happy and you know it, jump right up.
If you're happy and you know it, turn around.
If you're happy and you know it, take a bow.
If you're happy and you know it, say amen.

Children will enjoy suggesting their own words and motions.

I–10   JIMMY CRACK CORN   Grades K–3

Children hold up or point to the body parts indicated in the song.

Objectives: To hold up or point to body parts as they are called. To distinguish right and left.

Formation: An individual activity which may be done standing in front of or beside student desks.

Jimmy Crack Corn

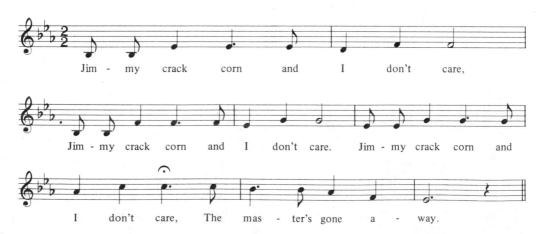

Verse 2:

Right hand up and I don't care, Right hand up and I don't care, Right hand up and I don't care, The master's gone away.

Verse 3:

Left hand up and I don't care . . .

Verse 4:

Right foot up and I don't care . . .

Verse 5:

Left foot up and I don't care . . .

Procedure:

1. Teach the first verse of the song.

2. Sing other verses and do what is indicated by the words. For example, on *Right hand up and I don't care*, students should raise the right hand, moving it in rhythm.

3. Different students can be called upon to supply new verses, with the rest joining in the song and doing the action after the first phrase. Possible verses are:

   Touch the left ear and I don't care.
   Wiggle your nose and I don't care.
   Blink your eyes and I don't care.
   Jump to the front and I don't care.
   Stoop and stand and I don't care.

You may have to supply a verse or two initially until the students understand what to do.

I–11   THE NOBLE DUKE OF YORK   Grades K–3

Motions illustrating the meaning of the words are done. This is a particularly good song for teaching and reviewing the concepts of "up" and "down."

Objectives: To move rhythmically with the music. To develop the meanings of the concepts "up" and "down" through appropriate motions on those words.

Formation: No special formation is required, but children need room to stand and stoop by or in front of their desks.

The Noble Duke of York

Verse 2

Oh, when you're up, you're up.
And when you're down, you're down.
But when you're only half way up,
You're neither up nor down.

Procedure:

1. Teach both verses of the song above. A brief discussion of the words of the song may be in order; for example, "Who is a Duke of York?"

2. Demonstrate the following motions as you sing the song again:

Hold up ten fingers on the phrase *He had ten thousand men.*

With hands about chest high in the front of the body, pretend to climb up (as though climbing a ladder) on the phrase *He marched them up to the top of the hill.*

Pretend to climb down with hands on the phrase *And he marched them down again.*

Reach up with arms extended above the head as far as possible (students need to be standing) on *Oh, when you're up, you're up.*

Stoop down on the phrase *Oh, when you're down, you're down.*

Come to a crouched position in which students are neither standing erect nor stooping on *But when you're only half way up, you're neither up nor down.*

After a demonstration of the above motions, invite students to do them with you as everyone sings the song. If there are any problems, go over the troublesome parts at a slower pace and then sing the entire song in the usual tempo.

3. If desired, develop the meaning of the number "ten thousand" with the children. Ask if anyone can write this number. If not, then write it yourself, asking students to count the number of zeros (four). Ask questions such as, "Do we have 10,000 students in this room? (No); "Do we have 10,000 students in the whole school? (No, more like 500–1000.) Depending upon how large your school is, you might tell then that it would take about ten or more schools to have 10,000 students.

Before the end of the period, erase the 10,000 that you wrote on the board, and see if several students can come to the board and write it.

I–12   WE'RE IN, RIGHT OUT   Grades K–3

Motions of this song illustrate the concepts of in-out and up-down.

Objectives: To perform the motions rhythmically. To illustrate through motions the concepts of in-out and up-down.

Formation: No special formaton is required; students should stand beside their desks.

We're in, Right Out

Procedure:

1. Demonstrate the above song, doing the motions as you sing. (The motions are outlined in step 2).

2. Before asking the children to sing the song and do the motions at the same time, practice just doing the motions while *saying* (not singing) the words at a slower tempo. The motions are as follows:

   We're in, right out, Touch the finger tips of both hands to your chest for "in," and then stretch arms out away from your body for "out."

   Right up, right down, Stretch arms upward, above the head on "up," and bring arms down on "down."

   We're happy all the time. Clap hands on the beat.

   We're in, right out, right up, right down. We're happy all the time. Repeat all of the above motions for these words.

   Since we came to school On the word "we" point to yourself and on the word "school" point to everyone else (or away from yourself).

   We've made a lot of friends. Point to others in the class, moving your hand rhythmically from left to right.

   We're in, right out, right up, right down, We're happy all the time. Repeat the above described motions for these same words.

   As soon as the children are able to do the motions in tempo, have them sing the song while doing them. It is important that they point in while singing "in," and point out while singing "out," etc.

3. Let children take turns leading the song as soon as they feel they are ready.

I–13   TEDDY BEAR   Grades K–3

This is a jump rope game in which individual children jump and do the motions mentioned in the song. At the end of the verse the jumper runs out and a new jumper runs in. It may also be used without the jump rope as an action song.

Objective: To jump rope and do the motions of the song simultaneously.

Equipment: A long jump rope.

Formation: An open space area large enough to accommodate a long jump rope is needed. Two children will turn the rope and a third child will run in to jump and perform the motions.

Teddy Bear

Ted - dy bear, Ted - dy bear, turn a - round,____

Ted - dy bear, Ted - dy bear, touch the ground. Ted - dy bear, Ted - dy bear,

show your shoe,____ Ted - dy bear, Ted - dy bear, that will do!

Verse 2

Teddy bear, Teddy bear, go upstairs.
Teddy bear, Teddy bear, say your prayers.
Teddy bear, Teddy bear, Switch off the light,
Teddy bear, Teddy bear, Say goodnight.

Procedure:

1. Teach both verses of the above song.
2. Ask what motions should be done with the words and when this is decided, do the motions as the verses are sung. Suggested motions are as follows:

Verse 1: *Turn around,* Everyone turns around.

Touch the ground. Do as the words say.

Show your shoe. Raise one foot and point to the shoe.

That will do! Shake your finger on each of the three words.

Verse 2: *Go upstairs.* Pretend to walk upstairs, using alternate feet.

Say your prayers. Assume a prayer stance by bringing your hands together about chin high and slightly bowing the head.

Switch off the light, Raise one hand above the head and then pull it down slightly as though grabbing a light cord and pulling it.

Say goodnight. Put your hands together and place them on one side of your tilted head as though going to sleep.

3. Tell students that they are going to do the motions, with a few changes while jumping rope. Select two students to turn the jump rope (a long rope about twelve to fifteen feet, not a single-person jump rope). Demonstrate doing the motions while jumping, or have another student (preferably one who has rehearsed beforehand) demonstrate. Jump rope motions for the above suggested motions are the same as those given above, with the selected jumper running in (if possible; if not, then stop the rope until he comes in and start the rope when the song begins). The jumper turns around, touches the ground, lifts one foot up and points (one-foot jumping is called for here), and shakes the finger on the first verse. On the second verse, the jumper should jump on alternate feet (emulating walking up the stairs), fold hands in a prayer stance, put one hand above the head to switch off the light, and then run out while the rope is still turning. Immediately, the next jumper runs in, ready to start the same set of motions over again while the class sings.

Variation:

Instead of singing *Teddy bear*, substitute students' names. Students whose names are used should do the motion that immediately follows. The same student's name should be used throughout a verse, with a different student's name substituted in the next verse. To challenge children, you might try changing children's names on each phrase, rather than on each verse. This activity may be done without using a jump rope.

I–14   THIS OLD MAN   Grades K–4

The correct number of fingers for each verse, going from one to ten, are held up and other indicated motions are performed.

Objectives: To move rhythmically to the music. To hold up the correct number of fingers for each verse.

Formation: No special formation is required.

This Old Man

This old man, he played one, He played nick nack on my thumb, with a

nick - nack, pad dy wack, Give a dog a bone. This old man came roll - ing home.

Verse 2:

This old man, he played two.
He played nick nack on my shoe.
With a nick nack, paddywack,
Give a dog a bone.
This old man came rolling home.
(Point to shoe)

Verse 3:

This old man, he played three,
He played nick nack on my knee . . .
(Point to knee)

Verse 4:

This old man, he played four,
He played nick nack on my door . . .
(Knock on desk)

Verse 5:

This old man, he played five,
He played nick nack on my hive . . .
(Pretend to shoo bees away)

Verse 6:

This old man, he played six.
He played nick nack on my sticks . . .
(Tap one index finger on the other one)

Verse 7:

This old man, he played seven.
He played nick nack up in heaven . . .
(Point to the sky)

Verse 8:

This old man, he played eight.
He played nick nack on my pate.
(Tap on your head)

Verse 9:

This old man, he played nine.
He played nick nack on my spine . . .
(Tap on your spine)

Verse 10:

This old man, he played ten.
He played nick nack once again . . .
(No motion)

Procedure:

1. Teach or review the above song by singing one or more verses.
2. Illustrate the motions to the first verse.

   Hold up one finger on the word "one"

   Hold out the thumb of one hand and tap it with the index finger of the other hand on the second phrase, which ends with the word *thumb.*

   On the third phrase, pat the upper legs with the hands twice on the words, *nick nack*, and clap twice on the word *paddywack.*

On the words *Give a dog a bone*, hold out one hand in front with the open palm facing up as though handing someone something.

On the words *This old man came rolling home*, roll one hand around the other.

After demonstrating the motions while singing the song, invite the children to try them with you. It may be necessary to slow the tempo until the children feel comfortable with the motions.

3. Teach the other verses, using the same motions except for the number of fingers held up for each number, and an appropriate motion for the last word in phrase two. Appropriate motions are indicated beside each verse.

4. It is important to check and see that children hold up the correct number of fingers on each verse.

Variations:

1. Instead of singing the numbers in order from one to ten, it is sometimes fun and challenging for the teacher to sing the first line as a solo, skipping around with the number. Children have to listen very carefully for the number sung in order to display the correct number of fingers before doing the accompanying motion. Generally, it is advisable to hesitate just a moment after singing the number word to give them time to display their fingers. At that point everyone then joins in the singing and continues to do the motions as outlined above.

2. As with most folk songs that have been around for a time, there are many different rhyming words and/or motions for the second phrase. There is nothing sacrosanct about these words and motions; invite children to make up other rhyming words and motions for each of the ten verses.

I–15   THE ANGEL BAND   Grades K–4

Children may hold up the appropriate number of fingers or stand as their number is sung and clap on the beat (or accent) during the refrain.

Objectives: To hold up the correct number of fingers as each number is sung. To stand or sit when a designated number is sung. To clap rhythmically on the beat or accent.

Formation: No special formation is required.

The Angel Band

There was one, there were two, there were three lit - tle an - gels. There were four, there were five, there were six lit - tle an - gels. There were sev'n, there were eight, there were nine lit - tle an - gels. Ten lit - tle — an - gels in the band. ———— Was - n't that a band, Sun - day morn - ing, Sun - day morn - ing, Sun - day morn - ing? Was - n't that a band, Sun - day morn - ing, Sun - day morn - ing soon? ————

Procedure:

1. Teach or review the above song.

2. Ask students to hold up the correct number of fingers as each number is sung in the verse. Look around to determine that students are accurate in the number of fingers. If they are not, it may be necessary to slow the song down.

3. Have them clap on the beat during the chorus.

4. Announce that you are going to check to see how well they count and listen by doing a different activity with the same song. Number the students by having them count off from one to ten. If there are more than ten students in the class, the eleventh student will start over again with one, as will also the twenty-first student. Therefore, in a class of thirty-four students, there would be four number 1's, four number 2's, four number 3's, four number 4's, but only three number 5's (this will be true for five through ten). When singing the verse through, all the number 1's stand when *one (There was one,)* is sung, all the number 2's stand when *two* is sung, and so on. On the refrain, all students should be standing as they clap on the beat. While there is no repeat given in the music, when this activity is done, it is generally a good idea to go back to the beginning of the verse and repeat it so that all students can sit down when their numbers are sung. The song can end after singing the verse the second time, or, if desired, the refrain can be repeated also.

Variation:

As this song concerns a band of angels, why not make it a real band. Call ten students to the front of the class and let them each choose one rhythm instrument to play. Be sure that two people standing next to each other do not have the same kind of instrument. Assign each of the ten students a number from one to ten (going from left to right as a child would read or write). Ask each child to play his instrument on the number he was assigned as it is sung. You or the student leader may need to cue each student at first. On the refrain, all students with instruments will play on the beat as they march briskly around the classroom with student number 1 as the leader. If there is time, assign new students the numbers from one to ten, and do the exercise again with them. All the other students should sing, put up the correct number of fingers on the verse, and clap on the refrain.

I–16   I KNOW A LITTLE PUSSY   Grades K–4

Children gradually rise and stoop according to the upward or downward movement of the tune. At the end children suddenly jump from crouched position as they say *Scat!*

Objective: To move gradually upward or downward according to the movement of the notes in the music.

Formation: No special formation is required. Children need ample room to stoop and jump in front of or beside their desks.

I Know a Little Pussy

I know a lit - tle pus - sy, ___ Her coat is sil - v'ry gray. ___ She

lives down in the mead - ow ___ not ver - y far a - way. ___ She'll

al - ways be a pus - sy, ___ She'll nev - er be a cat, ___ For

she's a pus - sy wil - low. ___ Now what do you think of that?

Meow, meow, meow, meow, meow, meow, meow, meow, *Scat!*

Procedure:

1. Ask the students to listen as you sing the song above to determine whether the notes go up or down. After listening they should respond that they went up at the beginning and then down on the *Meows.*

2. Tell the students that you would like them to join you in singing it (as much as they can; put the words on the blackboard or a chart) and doing the motions, which follow the movement of the notes in the song. As the song starts low and goes upward, they are to start low, or in a stooped position, and gradually get higher and higher until the phrase *And what do you think of that?* where they should be standing erect with arms stretched upward. On the *Meows,* which come down on a C scale, students should gradually return to their stooped positions, getting

softer and softer in volume. On the word *Scat!* they jump up suddenly and shout it so that someone who has not heard the song will be surprised by the last word.

3. Sing the song and do the motions with different parts of the class (half, one row, boys or girls) while the others listen to evaluate the performance.

Variation:

Instead of stooping and stretching to sing the song, students may use their hands to indicate the level of the pitch. They still jump up and shout when saying *Scat!*

I–17   HEAD, SHOULDERS, KNEES, AND TOES   Grades K–6

As each body part is sung, students touch that part. On successive repeats of the song, an additional word is omitted in the singing though students continue pointing to each body part.

Objectives: To move rhythmically as each named body part is touched. To think some parts of the song and enter at the proper place on the parts that are to be sung.

Formation: No special formation is required. Each student should have enough space to bend over and touch his toes and other body parts.

Head, Shoulders, Knees, and Toes

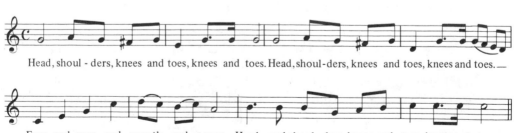

Head, shoul - ders, knees and toes, knees and toes. Head, shoul-ders, knees and toes, knees and toes. —

Eyes and ears and mouth _ and _ nose, Head and shoul - ders, knees and toes, knees and toes.

Procedure:

1. Sing the song above and do the motions, which consist of touching each body part as it is named.

2. Invite children to sing and do the motions with you. It may be necessary to slow the song down so they can locate each body part in order. Sing it two or three times until they feel comfortable with the song and motions.

3. Tell them they are going to do something special with the song this time. No one is to sing the word *Head* aloud. Instead they are to think it in their minds and touch their heads as they did before. The remainder of the song is sung as it normally is.

4. After leaving out the word *Head*, on the next repeat of the song, tell them to leave out *Head* and *shoulders*. They are to think these words as if they were singing and to continue pointing to those body parts. The first audible word in this verse should be *knees*.

5. The song should be repeated two more times, omitting an additional word each time so that on the last repeat, all four of the words, *Head, shoulders, knees, and toes* are thought instead of sung while the motions are being done. Students continue singing the middle part, *Eyes and ears and mouth and nose* on all repeats.

I–18   CABIN IN THE WOOD   Grades K–4

Children do the indicated motions illustrating the words of the song.

Objective: To perform the motions in a rhythmic manner.

Formation: No special formation is required.

Cabin in the Wood

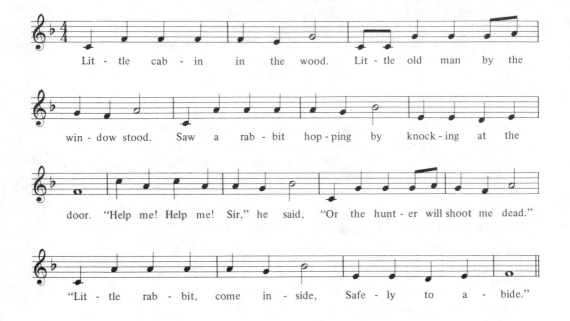

Lit - tle cab - in   in   the   wood.   Lit - tle old   man   by   the

win - dow stood.   Saw   a   rab - bit   hop - ping   by   knock - ing   at   the

door. "Help me! Help me! Sir," he   said,   "Or   the   hunt - er   will shoot me   dead."

"Lit - tle   rab - bit,   come   in - side,   Safe - ly   to   a - bide."

Procedure:

1. Teach or review the song above.

2. Teach the motions with the song. They are:

   Little cabin in the wood, Touch open fingertips together in front of your chest, making the outline of a cabin roof line (upside down vee).

Little old man by the window stood. Put the side of your hand above your eyes as though shading them (or saluting), trying to view something from a distance.

Saw a rabbit hopping by   Make a vee with the index and third fingers of each hand (other fingers and thumb are folded in a fist) to make rabbit ears; Move the hands in a bouncing motion across the front of the body as though a rabbit was hopping.

Knocking at the door. Pretend to knock on a door.

"Help me! Help me! Sir," *he said,* Thrust the hands up each time *"Help me!"* is sung, as though desperate for help.

"Or the hunters will shoot me dead," Close all the fingers into a fist except for the index finger, which should be pointing outward to imitate a gun.

"Little rabbit, come inside, safely to abide." Hold out the left hand and stroke it with the right hand as though soothing the upset rabbit.

To encourage good expressive singing, it would be helpful to discuss the meaning of the words of the song, emphasizing the feelings of the various characters in each portion. Invite various students to demonstrate how they would sing certain portions. Afterwards, let the class decide which way they like best and then sing the entire song through.

Variation:

Select students to play the role of each character in the song (the little old man, the rabbit, and the hunter) while the class sings it.

I–19   BINGO   Grades 1–6

Each time the song is repeated, a letter in the spelling of B I N G O is omitted in the singing and a clap is substituted so that on the sixth time through only five claps are heard where B I N G O would normally be sung.

Objective: To substitute a clap for the name of an additional letter in each repeat of the song.

Formation: No special formation is required. The class can sit or stand while performing this song with its motions.

Bingo

There was a farm-er had a dog and Bin-go was his name-o.

B - I - N - G - O,   B - I - N - G - O,

B - I - N - G - O   and Bin-go was his name-o.

Procedure:

1. Teach the above song.

2. After the children learn it, sing it through six times. The first time it should be sung as it is written. The second time, instead of singing *B* each of the three times *Bingo* is spelled, clap. Students immediately come back in singing on the second letter *I*. The third time, two letters, *B* and *I*, should be omitted in the singing with students clapping instead. Everyone should resume singing on the letter *N*. The song continues in this fashion with an additional letter being dropped each time the song is repeated, until all five letters in *Bingo* are clapped instead of sung.

I-20   WID MINE HANDS ON MINESELF   Grades 1-4

Key words and motions are cumulative in this little Dutch song as new verses are sung.

Objective: To perform cumulative words and motions in correct sequence.

Formation: Students should stand by their desks to perform this activity.

Wid Mine Hands on Mineself

Wid mine hands on mine-self, But vat is das here? Das is mine head think-er, mine ma-ma dear. Head think-er, head think-er, Nick-y, nick-y noo. Das vat I learned in das school._____

Verse 2:

Wid mine hands on mineself, But vat is das here?
Das is mine eye blinker, mine mama dear.
Eye blinker, head thinker, Nicky, nicky noo.
Das vat I learned in das school.

Verse 3:

Wid mine hands on mineself, but vat is das here?
Das is mine nose blower, mine mama dear.
Nose blower, eye blinker, head thinker (An extra measure identical to measure ten will be added here).
Das vat I learned in das school.

Verse 4:

(Line one is identical to those above.)
Das is mine yak yakker, mine mama dear.
Yak yakker, nose blower, eye blinker, head thinker
(two additional measures just like measure ten will be required here.)
(Line four is identical to those above.)

Verse 5:

Das is mine ear flapper, mine mama dear (Line two).
Ear flapper, yak yakker, nose blower, eye blinker, head thinker. . .

Verse 6:

Das is mine chest protector, mine mama dear.
Chest protector, ear flapper, yak yakker, nose blower, eye blinker,
head thinker. . .

Verse 7:

Das is mine bread basket, mine mama dear.
Bread basket, chest protector, ear flapper, yak yakker, nose blower,
eye blinker, head thinker . . .

Verse 8:

Das is mine knee bender, mine mama dear.
Knee bender, bread basket, chest protector, ear flapper, yak yakker,
nose blower, eye blinker, head thinker . . .

Verse 9:

Das is mine toe pointer, mine mama dear.
Toe pointer, knee bender, bread basket, chest protector, ear flapper,
yak yakker, nose blower, eye blinker, head thinker . . .

Procedure:

1. Sing three or four verses of the above song with the motions for the students so that they understand the cumulative quality of the verses. The motions are explained in the next step.

2. List the cumulative words on the blackboard:

   head thinker
   eye blinker
   nose blower
   yak yakker
   ear flapper
   chest protector
   bread basket
   knee bender
   toe pointer

   Explain that each time one of the above body parts is mentioned they are to point to it.

   Other motions that accompany the song are as follows:

   Wid mine hands on mine self, With a flourish, gradually place the hands on the hips.

But vat is das here? Point to the new body part mentioned in each verse; point to the forehead in verse 1, the eye in verse 2, the nose in verse 3, and so on.

Das is mine head thinker, mine mama dear. Point to the named body part in the different verses.

Head thinker, head thinker. Point to the named body parts, which are cumulative in subsequent verses.

Nicky, nicky, noo. Clap hands together lightly in the rhythm of this passage.

Das vat I learned in das school. Put one hand on the hip and shake the index finger on the opposite hand on the beat.

3. Invite the students to sing the song (all verses) with you. It may be necessary to stop occasionally and rehearse some parts as the words in subsequent verses continue to accumulate.

I–21   DO YOUR EARS HANG LOW?   Grades 2–6

This is a simple action song with indicated motions for each phrase.

Objective: To move rhythmically as the song is performed.

Formation: No special formation is required for this song. The children should stand throughout.

Do Your Ears Hang Low?

Do your ears hang low, do they wob-ble to and fro? Can you

tie them in a knot, can you tie them in a bow? Can you

throw them o-ver your shoul-ders like a con-ti-nen-tal sol-dier? Do your ears hang low?

Procedure:

1. Teach or review the above song.

2. Following are suggested motions that can be done with the song:

   Do your ears hang low, Extend both hands downward, with palms toward the floor, and move them to the beat.

   Do they wobble to and fro? With hands in the same position as above, move hands from side to side.

   Can you tie them in a knot, Roll your hands around each other at about waist level as though tying a knot.

   Can you tie them in a bow? Stop the rolling motion above and move each hand toward the outside of the body as though tightening each side of a bow.

   Can you throw them over your shoulders Wave each hand over its respective shoulder.

   Like a Continental soldier? Salute with the right hand.

   Do your ears hang low? Extend both hands downward with palms toward the floor, and move them on the beat.

3. Ask the students to try the motions with you. You may have to sing the song two or three times for them to coordinate the motions with the words. It is important that the motions be done rhythmically.

4. After the song is learned well, and preferably on a subsequent day, students might be asked to make up another verse, such as *Do your ears hang high?*

I-22   LITTLE BUNNY FOO FOO   Grades 2-6

This activity tells a story through choral speaking and a recurring chorus, which is sung. The activity ends with a surprising moral.

Objective: To portray the story through rhythmic movement, expressive choral speaking, and singing.

Formation: Students may remain seated while doing this activity.

Little Bunny Foo Foo

Verse 2:

*Little Bunny Foo Foo
I don't want to see you
Scooping up the field mice
And bopping them on the head.*

Procedure:

1. Teach both verses of the above song.
2. Tell the group that you would like their help in performing "Little Bunny Foo Foo." They are to sing verses one and two after you (the leader) do some speaking parts between the verses. The script is as follows:

   Sing verse 1.

   (Spoken) *Down came the good fairy, and she said:*
            (Use expression and body motions that are appropriate)

Sing verse 2.

(Spoken) *I will give you three chances, and then I will turn you*
        into a goon.

Sing verse 1.

(Spoken) *Down came the good fairy again, and she said:*

Sing verse 2.

(Spoken) *I will give you two more chances, and then I will turn*
        you into a goon.

Sing verse 1.

(Spoken) *Down came the good fairy again, and she said:*

Sing verse 2.

(Spoken) *Little Bunny Foo Foo, I will give you just one more*
        chance, and then I will turn you into a goon!

(Spoken) *Well, Little Bunny Foo Foo, just could not stand it,*
        Soooooooooo . . .

Sing verse 1.

(Spoken) *Down came the good fairy, and she said,*
        "Little Bunny Foo Foo, I gave you three chances!
        Now I am going to turn you into a goon!"
        ----- POOOOOOOOOOOOFFFFFFFFFFF -----

(Spoken) *And the moral of this story is:*

                Hare today, goon tomorrow!

3. While singing verses 1 and 2, invite students to do these motions with the words:

Make rabbit ears with the index and third fingers of each hand and move both hands to simulate hopping during the first half of each verse.

On the line *Scooping up the field mice*, make a scooping motion as though catching mice with the hands.

On the last line, *And bopping them on the head*, clench the left hand into a fist and strike the open palm of the right hand with it.

4. Perform the entire activity, with the leader doing the speaking parts between the verses and the group singing the verses and doing the motions.

5. Even though the ending will no longer be a surprise after the first performance, the group will enjoy performing this activity many times. For variation, some of the students may enjoy doing the spoken parts.

I–23   ONE FINGER, ONE THUMB, KEEP MOVING   Grades 2–6

The students begin this song in a seated position and do the motions indicated by the words of the song. An additional motion is done on each repeat of the song.

Objective: To sing the cumulative motion words in sequence and to do the movements rhythmically.

Formation: Students begin this game seated at their desks, but will need to stand and sit freely during the several repeats of the cumulative verses.

One Finger, One Thumb, Keep Moving

Each of the following verses are cumulative, with the results that the music may have to be modified to accommodate the additional words. This is illustrated for verse two.

Verse 2:

One finger, one thumb, one arm, keep moving,
One finger, one thumb, one arm, keep moving,
One finger, one thumb, one arm, keep moving,
We'll all be merry and bright.

Verse 3:

One finger, one thumb, one arm, one leg, keep moving . . .

Verse 4:

One finger, one thumb, one arm, one leg, one nod of the head, keep moving . . .

Verse 5:

One finger, one thumb, one arm, one leg, one nod of the head, stand up, sit down, keep moving . . .

Verse 6:

One finger, one thumb, one arm, one leg, one nod of the head, stand up, turn round, sit down, keep moving . . .

Procedure:

1. Teach verse one of the above song, doing the indicated motions of moving one finger (usually the right index finger) and one thumb (on the same hand as the moving finger). Repeat this verse at least twice or until the students are comfortable with the song. If they cannot sing this first verse well, they will have trouble with the remaining verses. Students are seated when they begin this song.

2. Sing the second verse with the group, calling to their attention that the verse is the same except for the addition of one other body part which is to move. As they sing the first phrase, they are to start moving each body part as it is mentioned. After each part begins to move, it continues moving until the end of the verse.

3 Sing the third verse with the group. Again, call their attention to the fact that this verse is just like the second verse except for the addition of another body part—one leg. As in the second verse, each body part begins to move as it is mentioned in the first phrase and continues moving until the end of the verse. All other verses are sung in the same way. Call special attention to the last verse where the addition is inserted in the middle of verse five's motion:

Verse 5:

One finger, one thumb, one arm, one leg, one nod of the head, stand up, sit down, *keep moving . . .*

Verse 6:

One finger, one thumb, one arm, one leg, one nod of the head, stand up, turn around, sit down, *keep moving . . .*

I–24   ABE LINCOLN HAD MANY SONS   Grades 2–6

This song features cumulative motions that are added at the end of each repeat of the song. All the cumulative motions continue simultaneously during the song. For instance, on the second verse, students will move only the right arm up and down. On the last verse, they will move the right and left arms up and down, march with both feet (in place), nod the head, and turn around simultaneously and in rhythm while they sing.

Objective: To do the cumulative motions in rhythm.

Formation: No special formation is required. The children will need
to stand.

Abe Lincoln Had Many Sons

Procedure:

1. Teach the above song.

2. After students know it well, put the following cumulative motions with the song:

   a. Move right forearm up and down in rhythm to the music.

   b. Move left forearm up and down in rhythm to the music.

   c. Move right foot up and down in rhythm.

   d. Move left foot up and down in rhythm as though marching.

   e. Nod the head up and down in rhythm.

   f. Turn around throughout the entire verse.

After the first verse, the group will say in rhythm, *Right arm* while moving the right arm up and down in rhythm. They repeat the song again, continuing to move the right arm up and down in rhythm. At the end of the first repeat of the song, students repeat *right arm* and add *left arm* right after it in this fashion:

They continue to move their right and left arms rhythmically in an alternating up and down direction while singing the song the third time. At the end of the third repeat, students say, *right arm, left arm, right foot,* one word per beat, and they move the body part mentioned. On the fourth repeat of the song, all three of these body parts move simultaneously. The song continues in this fashion with one additional body movement being added each time until all six of the movements listed earlier (a through f) in procedure step two are done simultaneously.

I-25   MY HAT IT HAS THREE CORNERS   Grades 2-6

Students do the indicated motions on certain words. The song is then repeated with the motion words omitted in the singing while children continue doing the motions.

Objective: To gradually substitute motions for the singing of certain designated words.

Formation: No special formation is required. Children should stand while singing and doing the motions of this song.

My Hat It Has Three Corners

Camp Song

Procedure:

1. Teach the above song without the motions.

2. Add the motions to the song. They are as follows:

   Point to yourself each time the word *my* occurs.

   Point to your head each time the word *hat* is sung.

   Hold up three fingers on the right hand each time the word *three* is sung.

   Bend the left elbow so that the forearm is pointing upward and point to the left elbow with the right index finger each time the word *corners* is sung.

   Practice singing the song with the motions until the class seems comfortable with it.

3. After the children feel comfortable singing the song with the motions, tell them that they are going to do something a little different with the song. Each time they come to one of the four motion words mentioned above (*my, hat, three, corners*), they are to omit singing those words and instead do just the motions. All other words are sung aloud.

4. When some of the children feel comfortable with the song, call upon one or more to lead it.

I-26   GUESS THE PATTERN   Grades 2-6

Short and long dashes, representing the rhythmic pattern of the first phrases of several listed songs are placed on the blackboard or a chart. The children guess what rhythmic pattern represents the beginning of an identified song.

Objective: To guess which of several rhythmic patterns, illustrated by dashes of varying lengths, is that of a specified well-known song.

Formation: No special formation is required. The students may remain in their seats.

Procedure:

1. On the blackboard or chart paper place three or more patterns of dashes of varying durations to represent the rhythm of the beginning phrases of three or more well-known songs. Below are the patterns for three such songs:

    A. "This Old Man"

        – – — – – — – – – – – –

        (*This old man, he played one,*
        He played nick-nack on my thumb)

    B. "It's a Small World After All" (Chorus)

        —— – – — —— – —

        (*It's a small world after all*)

    C. "Silent Night"

        —— – – —— —— – – ——

        (*Silent night, Holy night*)

    Only the patterns of dashes numbered sequentially should be written on the blackboard. Do not write the title of the song or the first phrases. This is the information the students are to supply.

2. Call students' attention to the several patterns of dashes on the board and state that they represent the rhythm of the beginnings of several familiar songs. Indicate that you are going to sing the beginning phrase of one song and they have to guess whether it is the rhythm indicated by dash pattern number one, two, or three.

3. Sing or play one of the beginning phrases (see Step one for the portion to sing). Ask the group which dash pattern they selected. Confirm the correct answer. Tell them not to reveal their next answer until you call for them to hold up the number of fingers that correspond with the selected dash pattern on the blackboard. Sing another song's beginning phrase. Remind them not to reveal their answers as they check the blackboard to select the correct number. Next, have them close their eyes as they hold up the number of fingers that show their answers. Confirm the correct answer.

4. Change the procedure for the last pattern. Sing a beginning phrase for a song that may or may not be the one represented by the remaining phrase dash pattern. The students must decide whether the dash pattern represents the sung phrase or not. If you use closed eyes and upraised fingers to indicate the answer, the class should decide on a code, such as one finger for yes and two fingers for no.

5. Other dash patterns that may be used for this activity are as follows:

A. "Yankee Doodle"

   _ _ _ _ _ _ _ _ _ _ _ — -

   (*Yankee Doodle went to town a riding on a pony*)

B. "All Night, All Day"

   ___ ___ _ - ___ _ _ _ _ _ _ _ — —

   (*All night, All day, Angels watching over me, my Lord*)

C. "America"

   _ _ _ ___ _ —

   (*My Country 'Tis of Thee*)

I–27   CUCKOO SONG   Grades 2–6

On the chorus, students do a three-beat motion pattern of slapping upper legs, clapping hands, and snapping fingers. On subsequent repeats of this chorus, the word *Cuckoo* is sung one additional time until it is repeated five times. The rhythmic pattern is adjusted so that on each *Cuckoo* that is sung, the fingers snap once.

Objectives: To perform the three-beat motion pattern rhythmically. To increase the number of *cuckoo's* sung without breaking the rhythmic pattern on each successive repeat of the chorus.

Formation: No specific formation is required. Students should stand to do these motions.

Cuckoo Song

English by
K. F. Rohrbough

Oh, I went to Pe-ter's flow-ing stream, Where the wa-ter's so clear, And I heard there the cuck-oo, as he sang from the wood.— Ho-lee-ah, Ho-lee-ah, kee-kee-ah, ho-lee-ah, cuck-oo. Ho-lee-ah, kee-kee-ah, ho-lee-ah, cuck-oo. Ho-lee-ah, kee-kee-ah, Ho-lee-ah, cuck-oo. Ho-lee-ah, kee-kee-ah, ho.—

From *Around the World in Two Hours.* Copyright © 1951.
World Around Songs. Used by permission.

Procedure:

1. Teach the above song. Pronounce the words in the chorus phonetically. Actually, only the chorus has to be taught to perform the activities suggested in the following steps.

2. Teach these motions with the chorus:

   On the first word of the chorus *Holeeah,* alternately slap both hands on the upper thighs in front of the body emulating a fast drum roll.

Throughout the remainder of the chorus, do this three motion pattern with each motion occurring on the beat:

Beat one of each measure: Slap hands on the upper thighs.

Beat two of each measure: Clap hands together.

Beat three of each measure: Snap fingers with both hands (or point the thumbs over their respective shoulders).

3. After students have learned the song (particularly the chorus) well with the motions, challenge them with the suggestion that they are to sing *cuckoo* twice each time it occurs in the chorus. This will necessitate a change in the motions as there needs to be a snap on each *cuckoo*. Below is the music to the chorus with this suggestion incorporated.

Ho - lee - ah, Ho - lee - ah, kee-kee - ah, ho - lee - ah, cuck - oo, cuck - oo.
Roll hands on thighs, Slap,   Clap,   Snap,   Slap,   Clap,   Snap,   Snap,

Ho - lee - ah, kee-kee - ah, ho - lee - ah, cuck-oo, cuck-oo. Ho - lee - ah, kee- kee - ah,
Slap   Clap,   Snap,   Slap,   Clap,   Snap,   Snap,   Slap,   Clap,   Snap,

Ho - lee - ah, cuck - oo, cuck - oo. Ho - lee - ah, kee - kee - ah, ho.
Slap,   Clap,   Snap,   Snap,   Slap,   Clap,   Snap,   Slap.

4. After singing two *cuckoos* each time the word occurs in the chorus, have them sing three *cuckoos* (on each *cuckoo*, they should snap fingers) and adjust the motion pattern on each measure where the *cuckoos* occur so the motions would be:

Slap thighs, clap hands, snap, snap, snap.

Continue to increase the number of *cuckoos* on each repeat of the chorus until the total number reaches five.

5. After the class understands what to do on the subsequent repeats of the song, sing the entire song all the way through. They should begin with the verse and then sing the chorus five times (without the verse), increasing the number of *cuckoos* on each repeat. When they are comfortable with the song, try speeding up the last repeat of the chorus where the five *cuckoos* are sung.

I–28   JOHN JACOB JINGLE
HEIMERSCHMIDT   Grades 3–6

Each time this song is repeated, it is sung softer until the singers only "think" the tune. The last phrase, however, is always sung at top volume. The trick is to sing this last phrase together on the same pitch even when the tune to the first part of the song is not audible.

Objectives: To keep accurate time and to remember pitch so that after a period of "silent singing" the group enters together at the designated place. To demonstrate knowledge of soft and loud in singing.

Formation: No special formation is required. Students sit or stand.

John Jacob Jingle Heimerschmidt

Procedure:

1. Teach the above song so that it is known well.

2. After the group learns the song, instruct them to keep repeating the song over and over. Each time it is repeated, the song should be a little softer until the group just thinks the tune (there is no audible sound). This procedure is true for the entire song except for the last phrase, *da da da da da da da da* on each repeat. This is sung as loudly as possible in contrast to the rest of the song. The fun comes when the song is barely audible or totally inaudible, to see if everyone enters on the last phrase at the proper time on the proper pitch.

I-29   LITTLE PETER RABBIT HAD
A FLEA UPON HIS EAR   Grades 3–6

Motions are assigned to key words, which are omitted in subsequent repeats of the song, though the motions continue.

Objective: To make the appropriate motion at the right time whether the key word is sung or just thought.

Formation: Students may stand or sit, as they please.

Little Peter Rabbit Had a Flea upon His Ear

Lit-tle Pe-ter Rab-bit had a flea up-on his ear, Lit-tle Pe-ter Rab-bit had a

flea up-on his ear, Lit-tle Pe-ter Rab-bit had a

flea up-on his ear, And he brushed it and it flew a-way.

Procedure:

1. Teach the above song without the motions.

2. Add the following motions to the song:

   Little Peter Rabbit Make rabbit ears by holding up the first and second fingers of each hand and hold them on the top of your head (They can be moved rhythmically as you sing).

   Had a flea Hold the thumb and first finger of one hand close to each other to indicate a very small flea.

   Upon his ear, Point to one ear.

   And he brushed it and it flew away. Brush the ear with one hand.

3. After students have seen you demonstrate the motions with the song as it is sung, invite them to join in. They may need to sing it several times before they feel comfortable with the motions.

4. After they've learned the song, have them sing it through five times. The first time through they will sing all the words and do all the motions. The second time through they should not sing the words *Little Peter Rabbit* while continuing to do the motions. The third time through they should not sing the motion words in the first two phrases, but continue doing the motions at the appropriate time. On the fourth and fifth times the song is sung, one additional motion phrase is not sung, so that on the last verse, the entire verse is not sung. The words are "thought" in rhythm as the motions are performed at the appropriate places.

I–30   JOHN BROWN'S FLIVVER HAD A PUNCTURE IN THE TIRE   Grades 3–6

Key words are represented by certain motions. On subsequent repetitions of the song, an additional key word is not sung while students continue doing the motions.

Objectives: To be able to think the rhythm and pitch of the song when certain words are not sung. To do appropriate motions when these words are not sung.

Formation: No special formation is required. It is advisable for the students to stand beside their desks.

John Brown's Flivver Had a Puncture in the Tire

Procedure:

1. Teach the above song.

2. After the students learn the song, sing it through five times. The first time it should be sung as before. The second time through, the word *flivver* should not be sung, and students should substitute a cranking motion with one hand (remember the old Model A's that had to be hand-cranked?). The third time through, both the word *flivver* and the word *puncture* should be omitted. The hand cranking motion should be repeated for *flivver* and a hissing sound (ssst) made to imitate escaping air from the tire. The fourth time through, omit all the words mentioned above and do the suggested actions; also, omit *tire*, drawing a circle with the hand for the tire. The fifth and last time through, repeat all the aforementioned substitutions and omissions; also, omit *piece of gum*, and substitute a motion of pulling the gum back and forth from the mouth.

3. To give students an additional challenge, speed up the tempo of the entire song.

I–31   STODOLA PUMPA   Grades 3–6

Clapping on *Stodola* and stamping on *Pumpa* and *Pum* are featured in this catchy little chorus. The tempo can be accelerated after it is learned to further challenge the group.

Objective: To clap and stamp at designated times in rhythm.

Formation: Students may stand beside their desks to do this activity.

Stodola Pumpa

Czech Folk Song

Sto - do - la, sto - do - la, sto - do - la, pum - pa,

Sto - do - la, pum - pa, Sto - do - la, pum - pa, Sto - do - la, sto - do - la,

Sto - do - la pum - pa, Sto - do - la pum, pum, pum, pum, pum.

Procedure:

1. Teach the above chorus. The words may seem a little strange to students and you may want to explain that the verse (which is not included here) tells of a young man walking his girlfriend home after a village party. On the way home they stop at the water pump in the middle of town, which was frequented by villagers to obtain fresh water daily. (There was no such thing as running water in each home in those days.) The words of this chorus emulate the movement of the pump handle as they pump the cool refreshing water for a drink. The words are pronounced this way:

stō dō läh   Pŭm päh

2. After students are able to sing the chorus reasonably well, have them clap only on the word *stodola* using the same rhythm as the word (♫ ♩). They do nothing on the word *Pumpa* or *Pum* at this time. This is not quite as easy as it sounds as there

is a tendency to clap on the *pumpas* also. To practice, it might be advisable to divide the class into different sections to try it (boys–girls, each row, etc.)

3. After they are able to clap reasonably well on *Stodola*, ask them to omit the clapping and stamp only on the *Pumpa* or *Pum*. They should stamp on each syllable, which is always a quarter note.

4. When students can do steps two and three, ask them to combine the two as they sing the chorus: clap on *stodola*, and stamp on *pumpa* or *pum*. If the group has trouble putting the two motions together, slow down until they can.

5. To further challenge students, speed up the tempo. Divide the group into smaller groups to see which group can perform the best.

I-32   AN AUSTRIAN WENT YODELING   Grades 3-6

A combination of the slap-clap-snap movement and cumulative motions for the characters of the successive verses combine to make this song a challenging and enjoyable experience.

Objective: To perform the designated motions, including the cumulative motions in the successive repeats, in the correct order and in rhythm.

Formation: Students may stand beside their desks to perform this activity.

An Austrian Went Yodeling

Verses 2–5: Each verse is exactly the same, except for the word *avalanche*, which is changed to the following words in each successive verse. A corresponding motion word is added in the refrain (these motion words are cumulative as they are added).

Verse 2:   *Grizzly bear* (motion word is *Grrr*)

  3:     *St. Bernard* (motion words are *Arf, Arf*)

  4:     *Jersey cow* (motion words are *Swish, swish*)

  5:     *Pretty maid* (motion words are *Kiss, kiss*)

Procedure:

1. Teach the first verse to the above song. The words in the chorus have been written phonetically to aid in their pronunciation. It is advisable to do the words and the motions simultaneously, though it may be necessary to slow it down until students learn the chorus better. The motions for the refrain are as follows:

    a. On the first three notes with the fermatas (⌢) roll the hands (a fast slapping with alternate hands) on the upper legs.

    b. Slap hands on the front of the upper legs on the first beat of each measure in the refrain.

    c. Clap both hands together about chest level on beat two of each measure in the refrain.

d. Snap fingers of each hand (or point thumbs over their respective shoulders) on beat three of each measure of the refrain.

e. Do an appropriate motion for each motion word. On the word
Swoosh (representing the avalanche), place both hands side
by side with palms downward and move them in a downward

motion emulating falling snow in an avalanche. Other motions for the various motion words are as follows:

Grr: Place cupped hands in front or at about chest level in imitation of an animal's paws.

Arf, arf: Same position as above, but bark like a dog.

Swish, swish: Make a milking motion with the right and then the left hand (close hands as if grasping an udder and pull the right hand down, and then the left).

Kiss, kiss: These words will not be spoken; instead, students will pucker their lips and make two smacking sounds. Place hand on the waist.

2. It is important that the students be able to sing the first verse and refrain well before doing the successive verses. You should demonstrate the second verse before asking them to do it (it takes practice for the teacher, too, but it's worth it). The motions are cumulative, as are the motion words, so that the refrain for the second verse goes this way:

H–o–o–lee–ee–ee–ah–h–h.
Ho–lee–ah, kee–kee–ah, Ho–lee–ah, cuckoo, Swoosh, Grr.
Ho–lee–ah, kee–kee–ah, Ho–lee–ah, cuckoo, Swoosh, Grr.
Ho–lee–ah, kee–kee–ah, Ho–lee–ah, cuckoo, Swoosh, Grr.
Ho–lee–ah, kee–kee–ah, Ho–o–o.

3. Teach the remaining verses, keeping all the motion words and related motions in prior verses and adding new ones for each successive verse. The refrain to the last verse is as follows:

Ho - lee - ah, Ho - lee - ah, kee - kee - ah, ho - lee - ah, cuck - oo.

Swoosh, Grrr, Arf, Arf, Swish, Swish, Kiss, Kiss
(Spoken)

Ho - lee - ah, kee - kee - ah,

ho - lee - ah, cuck - oo. Swoosh, Grrr, Arf, Arf, Swish, Swish, Kiss, Kiss.

Ho - lee - ah, kee - kee - ah, ho - lee - ah, cuck - oo. Swoosh, Grrr, Arf, Arf,

Swish, Swish, Kiss, Kiss. Ho - lee - ah, kee - kee - ah, ho-o-o.

I–33   FOLLOW THE POINTER   Grades 3–6

Numbers from one to eight (or syllables from low do to high do) are arranged vertically, with eight at the top, on the blackboard. The leader points to a series of numbers, each one representing a step of the major scale, and children sing the tone represented by the number.

Objective: To sing the steps of the scale pointed to by the leader.

Formation: No special formation is required for this activity. Students may remain seated in their desks as long as they have a clear view of blackboard.

Procedure:

1. Write the numbers one through eight on the blackboard in a vertical column with one on the bottom and eight at the top. Syllables (do, re, mi, fa, sol, la, ti, do) could be used instead if desired.

2. Ask the group to sing a major scale, beginning on B flat or C, as you point to each number. If students are not familiar with the major scale, you should demonstrate it for them (all eight white notes on the piano, beginning with middle C and ending on the C an octave above). Practice this scale, going up and down, several times.

3. After singing the scale, change the pattern in step two by using progressions such as the ones suggested below:

   A. 1 2 3 2 1

   B. 1 2 3 4 5 4 3 2 3 2 1

   C. 1 2 3 4 3 4 5 6 7 6 7 6 7 6 6 5 4 3 2 1

4. After students are able to perform steps two and three in an acceptable manner, have them review the intervals of 1-3-5-8-5-3-1 with the pointer. Again, you may have to demonstrate these intervals, and perhaps sing with them at first.

5. Integrate the intervals in step four in subsequent exercises in which they are to sing the steps of the scale indicated by the pointer. Suggested exercises are:

   A. 1   3   5   8   5   3   1   2   3   4   5   4   3   2   1

   B. 1   2   3   4   5   6   7   8   5   3   1

   C. 1   3   5   4   3   2   1   5   1

6. Without announcing it beforehand, point to a succession of pitches that will produce a well-known tune and see if they recognize it. If they do not, tell them at the end and repeat the exercise so that they can listen for the tune. Tunes that may be used are listed below:

   A. "Hot Cross Buns"
      3-2-1---, 3-2-1--- (Each dash and number represent one beat)
      1111 2222 3-2-1---

   B. "Mary Had a Little Lamb"
      3212333-, 222-355-
      3212333322321---

   C. "Twinkle, Twinkle, Little Star"
      1155665-, 4433221-
      5544332-, 5544332-
      1155665-, 4433221-

II

SINGING ACTIVITIES AND GAMES FOR ONE OR MORE STUDENTS

This section is written for those who wish singing activities and games suitable for small groups. While they are designed primarily for groups of three to fifteen people, there is no reason why many cannot be performed with larger groups.

Generally, activities and games in this part will require more time and space to perform than those in Part I. Students (one or more—up to approximately fifteen) should move into a limited open space area away from their desks. Most of the activities can be performed in a time period of five to twenty minutes, depending upon the number of repetitions.

Again, these activities range from those that are very simple for elementary children to those that are more difficult. The very simple activities are appropriate for preschoolers as well as for primary grade children, and the more difficult ones are appropriate for students above elementary school age as well as those in the middle and upper elementary grades.

A wide variety of activities is represented in this part. Dramatization of words is the featured activity in "Little Miss Muffet," "Three Little Kittens," "Old Woman," "Daisy," and others. Games are featured in "Warmer or Colder," "Guess the Tune," "Tone Call Game," etc. Rhythmic physical movement is the key element in "Skip, Skip, Skip," "One Elephant," and "One Little Skeleton." Teachers and parents should be pleased to note that academic skill development is a prominent element in songs and activities such as "Guess the Number I'm Clapping," "B is for Bobby," "If Your Name Begins with the Letter You Hear," and "The Valentine."

Several repetitions of the activities may be required. The charm of a song such as "There Was an Old Woman Who Swallowed a Fly" lies in the cumulative repetition of certain words, phrases, and/or motions in subsequent verses. It is important that most, if not all, verses be performed.

Other songs that may have only one or two verses may be repeated to allow for a change in the student performers or "stars." "Three Little Kittens" may be repeated in its entirely two to four times, changing actors on each repetition. Each child in a class or group needs a chance to enjoy the limelight periodically!

Another group of songs that should be repeated are those lending themselves to practice or drill of an academic skill. By changing the letter sound featured in "If Your Name Begins with the Letter You Hear," repetitions can be used without boring the children.

Some of these activities may require some prior practice and preparation before using them with children; for example, "Nani Wale Na Hala" and "Tinikling," but most are quite simple and will require a minimum of preparation.

This mixture of familiar, not-so-familiar, traditional, and ethnic singing games and activities is presented for your pleasure. Enjoy them!

II–1   GUESS THE NUMBER
I'M CLAPPING   Grades K–1

The teacher claps or taps out a number from one to six and the students identify the number clapped by writing it on paper, holding up the correct number of fingers, or holding up a card with the numeral.

Objective: To identify the number of claps or taps heard.

Formation: Students should be seated at their desks.

Equipment: If students hold up fingers, no equipment is needed; if other variations of the activity are used, you may need pencils and paper, or cards on which numerals from one to six are written.

Procedure:

1. Clap out one number at a time from one to six. After each number is clapped, instruct the students to either hold up the number of fingers that match with the number clapped, or write down the appropriate number, or select the appropriate card from a set with numerals from one to six.

2. When students understand how the game is played, invite a student to be the leader, clapping out the numbers.

II–2   "B" IS FOR BOBBY   Grades K–1

Children identify the various letters of the alphabet, which are substituted in the song.

Objectives: To identify the written letter of the alphabet that is used in the song. To identify names of children that begin with an identified letter of the alphabet.

Formation: Children remain seated at their desks and respond by holding up a card with the correct answer.

Equipment: A set of twenty-six cards with a letter of the alphabet on each card for each child.

"B" Is for Bobby

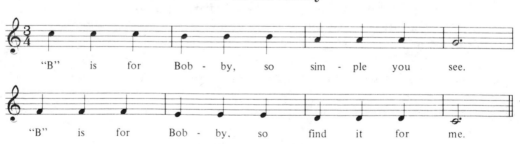

"B" is for Bob - by, so sim - ple you see.

"B" is for Bob - by, so find it for me.

Procedure:

1. Teach the song above.
2. Explain to the children that they are to find the letter "B" in their alphabet sets and hold it up.
3. Substitute another letter of the alphabet and a name that begins with that letter (the children may help do this if you desire), and the children find this letter and hold it up.
4. Continue substituting letters and names for the duration of the activity.

Variations:

1. Colors may be taught or reviewed using this song; for example, *"R" is for red, so simple you see. "R" is for red, so find it for me."* Each student should have a set of colored papers so they can select the appropriate color and hold it up.

2. Other concepts such as shapes and numbers can be used in the same manner as colors in Variation 1.

II–3   WHO'S THAT TAPPING
AT MY WINDOW?   Grades K–2

One child at a time selects an instrument (usually a rhythm instrument) and plays it without the other children seeing it, while the class sings. The class must guess the instrument selected.

Objective: To identify an instrument by hearing it played.

Formation: Except for the one selected child, the class remains seated at their desks. The instruments should be concealed behind a screen, room divider, or such, so that the class cannot see the instrument selected and played by the child.

Who's That Tapping at My Window?

American Folk Song

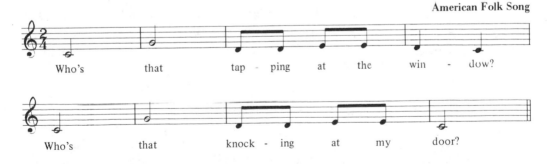

Who's   that   tap - ping   at   the   win - dow?

Who's   that   knock - ing   at   my   door?

Procedure:

1. Teach the above song.

2. Arrange several different instruments behind a screen, room divider, piano, or other barrier that a child can go behind. Choose a child to select an instrument and play it without being seen by the class. Instruments, such as rhythm instruments

(drum, triangle, tambourine, maracas, sticks, tone blocks, finger cymbals, claves, jingle sticks, jingle bells), song or tone bells, flutophone, or the like may be used. These instruments should be introduced to the class beforehand so that the students are familiar with the name of each one and the sound it makes.

3. Choose one child to go behind the barrier and select one instrument to play on the beat or accent.

4. The group sings while the child plays.

5. Ask someone in the class to identify the instrument played, or point to the names of the instruments that are written on the blackboard, and let the class members vote on the one they thought was being played.

6. Ask the child who played the instrument to come from behind the barrier and show the instrument that was played.

7. Sing the song through several times more, selecting a different student each time to go behind the barrier and play an instrument. The same procedure as outlined should be followed as many times as desired.

II–4   THREE BLUE PIGEONS   Grades K–2

This is a counting song, which may be dramatized by three students. The pigeons fly away, one at a time, and then return, one at a time.

Objective: To reinforce numbers from one to three and the principle of subtracting one and then adding one.

Formation: All the children are seated, except for the three who play the parts of the pigeons. One pigeon flies away on each verse until they are all gone. Then the pigeons return, one on each verse, until they are all back.

Three Blue Pigeons

Verse 2:

Two blue pigeons . . .

Verse 3:

One blue pigeon . . .

Verse 4:

No blue pigeons . . .

Before each of the verses above (two through four), you say "One flew away," and the class responds with a spoken "Oooh."

Verse 5:

One blue pigeon . . .

Verse 6:

Two blue pigeons . . .

Verse 7:

Three blue pigeons . . .

Before each of the verses above (five through seven), you say, "One flew back," and the class responds with a happy "Wheee."

Procedure:

1. Teach the song above.

2. Select three students to go to the front of the class and pretend they are pigeons. As you say, "One flew away" before verses two, three, and four, one student each time pretends to fly away by flapping her arms and going to a designated spot (outside the door, behind a bookshelf). As you say, "One flew back" before each of the verses five, six, and seven, the students "fly" back one by one until verse seven, when all three pigeons are back.

3. Coach the class on when to say their "Ooohs" and "Wheees" and the manner in which they are to say them.

Variations:

1. Instead of using students to dramatize the song, cut out three pigeons from blue construction paper and place them on the chalk trough. Remove and replace the pigeons as indicated by the song. After students understand the procedure, ask for volunteers to come up and manipulate the construction paper pigeons.

2. Change the color of the pigeons; for example, *Three red pigeons sitting on the wall.*

3. Change the number of pigeons. If larger numbers than three are being introduced, start with one of them. For instance, *Ten blue pigeons . . .* could be used. As it would take a good deal of time for all ten to fly away and return, perhaps only three or four might fly away before they start returning again.

II–5   JACK AND JILL   Grades K–2

This is a nursery rhyme, to be dramatized by two children, and sung by the entire class. It is brief enough to be performed several times.

Objective: To dramatize a nursery rhyme in a creative manner as it is sung.

Formation: All students remain seated except for the two, a boy and a girl, who play the roles of Jack and Jill in an open area in the front of the classroom.

Jack and Jill

Jack and Jill went up the hill to fetch a pail of wa - ter.

Jack fell down and broke his crown, And Jill came tum - bling af - ter.

Verse 2:

Up Jack got and home did trot.
   As fast as he could caper.
Went to bed to mend his head
   With vinegar and brown paper.

Procedure:

1. Teach the above song, using both verses.

2. Discuss the story told in the two verses. Several of the words, such as fetch, crown, caper, are not widely used today and may need explanation. Encourage children to use other words when relating the story of the song.

3. Line by line, discuss what movements would be appropriate in a pantomime. Encourage divergent ideas and emphasize the fact that those chosen to dramatize the song may use any of the discussed ideas or make up others as long as they are related to the ideas expressed in the words of the song.

4. Select two children, a boy and a girl, to come to the open space area to dramatize the song as the class sings it.

5. The song may be sung three or four times, using different children for the dramatizations each time.

II–6   THREE LITTLE KITTENS   Grades K–2

This is a nursery rhyme to be dramatized by four children, and sung by the class. It is brief enough to be performed several times.

Objective: To creatively dramatize a nursery rhyme as it is sung.

Formation: All students remain seated except for four children who play the roles of the three kittens and the mother cat in the open space area of the classroom.

Three Little Kittens

1. Three lit - tle kit - tens, they lost their mit - tens and they be - gan to cry.____ "Oh, moth - er, dear! We sad - ly fear Our mit - tens we have lost."____ "What, lost your mit - tens, you naught - y kit - tens, then you shall have no pie."____ Me - ow, me - ow, me - ow, meow.____

Verse 2:

Three little kittens they found their mittens
   And they began to cry.
"Oh, Mother dear! See here, see here,
   Our mittens we have found."
"What, found your mittens, you good little kittens,
   Then you shall have some pie."'
Meow, meow, meow, meow.

Procedure:

1. Teach or review "Three Little Kittens."

2. Announce that some members of the class will be asked to act out the above song. Ask what characters are needed (three kittens, Mother Cat).

3. Decide who will sing each phrase.

Phrase 1: *Three little kittens they lost their mittens and they began to cry.* (Entire class sings.)

Phrase 2: *"Oh, Mother dear, we sadly fear, our mittens we have lost!"* (Three kittens sing, or if desired, the entire class may sing it.)

Phrase 3: *"What lost your mittens, you naughty kittens, Then you shall have no pie."* (Mother Cat sings, or if desired, the entire class may sing it.)

Phrase 4: *Meow, meow, meow, meow.* (Three kittens sing, or if desired, the entire class may sing it.)

The four phrases in verse two are sung by the same characters as outlined for the first verse.

4. Discuss how each character feels in the different phrases in both verses and how the parts should be sung. Demonstrations may be called for here.

5. Select children from the class to play the three kittens and the mother cat. Sing the song several times, changing the characters each time.

II–7   LITTLE MISS MUFFET   Grades K–2

This is a nursery rhyme to be dramatized by two children, and sung by the entire class. It is brief enough to be performed several times.

Objective: To creatively dramatize a nursery rhyme as it is sung.

Formation: All students remain seated except for two children who play the roles of Little Miss Muffet and the spider in the open space area of the classroom.

Little Miss Muffet

Procedure:

1. Teach or review the above song.

2. Announce that some members of the class will be asked to act out the above song. Ask what characters are needed (Little Miss Muffet and the spider).

3. Discuss what is happening in the song and invite suggestions for acting out the song.

4. Select two students to play the roles while the class sings. Encourage appropriate expression on the part of each character. It may be necessary to have several students show how they think the parts should be played to "inspire" the selected actors.

5. Sing the song several times, changing the characters each time.

II–8   HICKORY DICKORY DOCK   Grades K–2

This is a nursery rhyme that can be dramatized, performed as an action song, and performed with instruments.

Objectives: To interpret the nursery rhyme by dramatizing it or doing the motions. To play rhythm instruments with the song.

Formation: The children can remain in their seats or stand by their seats except for the two who play the roles of the clock and the mouse.

Hickory Dickory Dock

Hick - o - ry dick - o - ry dock. *(Tick, tock)* The

mouse ran up the clock. *(Tick, tock)* The clock struck one, and

down he run. Hick - o - ry dick - o - ry dock. *(Tick, tock)*

Procedure:

1. Teach or review "Hickory Dickory Dock."

2. Discuss what is happening in the song and how actors from the class could portray the action.

3. Select two students, one to play the clock and one to play the mouse, to role play the song while the class sings it. Discuss alternate ways of portraying the mouse running up the clock (since it is not practical that one student should try to run over another) such as the mouse standing on one side pretending to run up the clock. Make sure the clock strikes "one" in some manner by clapping the hands or using an instrument.

4. The song may be sung several times, changing the actors each time.

Variations:

1. Instrumental accompaniment to this familiar song can enhance its performance as well as provide great pleasure for the performers. The following instruments are suggested for accompanying "Hickory Dickory Dock," but children may prefer to suggest their own instruments to be played in whatever manner they deem appropriate. While several instruments are suggested here, not all have to be used: for example, only two of the suggested instrumental accompaniments may be used.

a. The tone blocks or claves may be played on the *tick, tocks* in measures 2, 4, and 8.

b. Strike the drum or triangle on the word *one* to emulate the striking of the clock.

c. Play the octave "Cs" on the accents throughout the song as notated below:

While the tone bells may be started on the first word of the song, it is very effective to start them about two measures before the singing begins and to continue them two and a half measures after the last measure of the song, ending on the high "C."

2. "Hickory, Dickory, Dock" can simply be sung with the motions, which are as follows:

Hickory, Dickory, Dock. Rest the left elbow in the palm of the right hand and move the upper left arm back and forth after the fashion of a grandfather clock.

The mouse ran up the clock. Remove the right hand from beneath the left elbow and with the first two fingers pretend to "run" up the left upper arm, which is still in a vertical position.

The clock struck one, On the word *one*, clap both hands together.

And down he'd run. With the left upper arm restored to a vertical position, pretend to "run" it with the first two fingers of the right hand.

Hickory, Dickory, Dock. Place the palm of the right hand underneath the left elbow and move the left upper arm in a back and forth manner after the fashion of the pendulum of the grandfather clock.

II-9   FIVE LITTLE DUCKS WENT OUT TO PLAY   Grades K-2

Seven children dramatize the words to this song, which can also be done as a simple action song.

Objectives: To interpret the words of the song through dramatization. To move rhythmically while singing the song.

Formation: The children portraying the five ducklings and the mother duck occupy the center of the open space area initially. On the last verse, the father duck takes the mother duck's old position as she steps aside. The ducklings are required to move back and forth from home to the "hills," locations which should be designated before the singing begins. The other class members may remain in their seats and sing.

Five Little Ducks Went Out to Play

1. Five lit - tle ducks went out to play,
O - ver the hills and far a - way. The moth - er duck said, "Quack,
quack, quack, quack." Four lit - tle ducks came wad - dling back.

Verse 2:

Four little ducks went out to play
Over the hills and far away.
The mother duck said, "Quack, quack, quack, quack!"
Three little ducks came waddling back.

Verse 3:

Three little ducks went out to play . . .
Two little ducks came waddling back.

Verse 4:

Two little ducks went out to play . . .
One little duck came waddling back.

Verse 5:

One little duck went out to play . . .
No little ducks came waddling back.

Verse 6:

No little ducks went out to play.
Over the hills and far away.
The father duck said, "Quack, quack, quack, quack!
Five little ducks came waddling back!

Procedure:

1. Teach the above song, going through all the verses.

2. Discuss the meaning of the words with the children, and how they think Mother Duck called the little ducklings in from play. (Did she sound as though she meant it or not?) Ask if they think the father duck sounded any different? Have children demonstrate the difference in how the mother and father ducks sounded.

3. Select seven children to play the roles of the five ducklings, the mother duck, and the father duck. Help children plan the staging: where each is to stand, and when they "go out to play," where they go. Make sure Father Duck knows when to enter and that he knows the manner in which his "Quacks" are to be said. Also discuss the reentrance of all five duckings on the last verse (they will probably enter in a hurry).

4. The entire class should sing the song on all verses except for the *Quacks*, which are sung as a solo by the mother or father duck (unless the class decides otherwise).

5. If there is time, the class might enjoy singing the song one more time with a new cast of characters.

Variation:

This song can also be performed simply as an action song with children sitting or standing at their desks. The motions are as follows:

Phrase 1: *Five little ducks went out to play,* Hold up five fingers (or the appropriate number of fingers for the other verses), moving the hand rhythmically.

Phrase 2: *Over the hills and far away.* Move hand and arm in a semicircle as though outlining the tops of hills and then point to a distant place for "far away."

Phrase 3: *The mother duck said, "Quack, quack, quack, quack!* Place one hand on top of the other with palms facing each other and open and close the fingers to create the impression of a duck's bill opening and closing for the quacks.

Phrase 4: *Four little ducks came waddling back.* Hold up four fingers, moving the hand in rhythm to the music. (For subsequent verses, hold up the appropriate number of fingers.)

All six verses should be sung each time the song is performed. After the children are familiar with it, select one or two children to lead it.

II–10   TWO LITTLE BLACKBIRDS
SITTING ON A HILL   Grades K–2

A flannelboard with appropriate characters can be used by children to illustrate the meaning of the song, or children can dramatize the song.

Objective: To interpret the meaning of the song through dramatization or a flannelboard presentation.

Formation: All children are seated at their desks singing while one child manipulates the flannelboard characters, or, if dramatized, two children will need to come to the open space area.

Two Little Blackbirds Sitting on a Hill

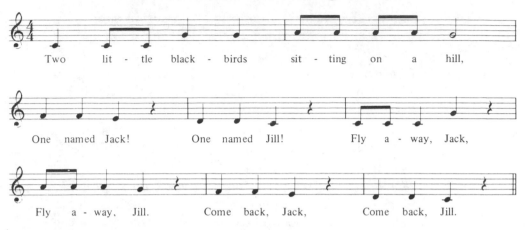

Two lit - tle black - birds sit - ting on a hill,

One named Jack! One named Jill! Fly a - way, Jack,

Fly a - way, Jill. Come back, Jack, Come back, Jill.

Procedure:

1. Teach or review the above song.

2. A flannelboard with two flannel blackbirds are needed for this presentation. Demonstrate the use of the flannel characters while the children sing.

3. Children may sing the song using these motions:

   Phrase 1: *Two little blackbirds sitting on a hill,* Hold up the index finger on each hand.

   Phrase 2: *One named Jack, one named Jill.* Wiggle one finger on the first half of the phrase, and the other finger on the second half of the phrase.

   Phrase 3: *Fly away, Jack! Fly away, Jill!* Flap one finger up and down, gradually make it "fly" away behind the back; flap the other finger up and down, gradually make it "fly" away behind the back.

   Phrase 4: *Come back, Jack, Come back, Jill.* One at a time and moving the fingers in a "flying" motion, bring the fingers back to the front of the body.

   After children are familiar with this song and the motions, select one or two children each time it is sung to act as leaders.

II–11   THE OLD GRAY CAT   Grades K–3

The words to this song tell a delightful story. It can be easily dramatized by children.

Objective: To interpret the meaning of this song through dramatization.

Formation: All the children are seated in their usual places except for the few who participate in the dramatization in the front of the room.

The Old Gray Cat

Traditional American Song

The old gray cat is sleep - ing, sleep - ing, sleep - ing. The

old gray cat is sleep - ing in the house.____

Verse 2:

The little mice are creeping, creeping, creeping.
The little mice are creeping through the house.

Verse 3:

The little mice are nibbling . . . in the house.

Verse 4:

The little mice are sleeping . . . in the house.

Verse 5:

The old gray cat comes creeping . . . through the house.

Verse 6:

The little mice all scamper . . . through the house.

Procedure:

1. Teach the above song, singing all the verses. Ask the children to pay particular attention to the meaning of the words.

2. Discuss with the children the action that is taking place in verses one through six. Focus on the verbs—creeping, nibbling, scamper—letting children demonstrate the actions that are inherent in the meanings of each one.

3. Select one child to be the cat and several to be the mice (this is a good opportunity to call attention to the singular and plural forms of this noun and their meanings; for example, if you're talking about only one of these animals, how would you spell the word? When you're talking about more than one, how would you spell the word? How many do we mean when we say "mice"? (We mean two or more.)

4. Depending upon the time available, this song may be performed one or more times, selecting a different cast for each performance.

Variation:

The children may be encouraged to make up a new set of words for a familiar experience that they can dramatize. Suggestions for such topics are shopping for groceries, a cooking experience, getting a haircut. Verses such as these help children understand the process involved in an activity and the sequencing attached to it:

Verse 1:

We like to bake some cookies, cookies, cookies.
We like to bake some cookies in the oven.

Verse 2:

We stir in flour and sugar, sugar, sugar.
We stir in flour and sugar and all the rest.

Verse 3:

We bake them in the oven, oven, oven.
We bake them in the oven, 'til they're brown.

Verse 4:

We like to eat the cookies, cookies, cookies.
We like to eat the cookies. Yum, they're good!

II–12   JACK O'LANTERN   Grades K–2

A simple Halloween song in which children take turns jumping
from behind a large Jack O'Lantern cutout to say or sing as a solo
the word *Boo!* at the end of the song.

Objectives: To participate in a Halloween song by singing or shout-
ing the word *Boo!* at the proper time with the proper expression. To participate in a beginning solo experience.

Formation: All the class members remain in their seats while singing, except for one, who hides behind a large Jack O'Lantern cutout in the front of the class until he jumps out
on the last word of the verse.

Jack O'Lantern

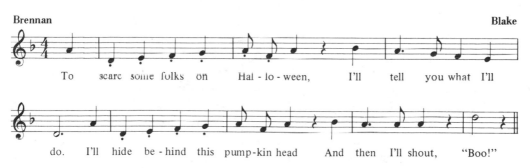

Brennan / Blake

To scare some folks on Hal-lo-ween, I'll tell you what I'll
do. I'll hide be-hind this pump-kin head And then I'll shout, "Boo!"

Procedure:

1. Teach the above song to the children.
2. A different child is selected each time it is sung to stand behind
   a large cutout of a Jack O'Lantern placed in the front of the
   class. The child selected jumps from behind the Jack O'Lantern
   on the last word of the song and sings it as a solo. Encourage
   him to sing and move with expression.

II–13   IT'S PICK-UP TIME   Grades K–3

A song to sing while children move around picking up papers, books, and so on, and putting them back in place. Rhythmic movement and cooperative work are emphasized.

Objective: To move rhythmically without bumping into others while neatly putting away things, or cleaning up.

Formation: No special formation is required, but children need to be reminded that they must be careful not to bump into others while doing the pick-up job.

It's Pick-Up Time

It's   pick - up   time,   It's   pick - up   time.   Put   ev - 'ry - thing   in   its

place.   It's   pick - up   time,   It's   pick - up   time,   It's   get - ting   neat - er   now.

Procedure:

1. Teach the above song.

2. Tell children that this is an excellent song to sing when things need to picked up or straightened, and that singing while working makes it more fun. Stress the importance of not running or bumping into anyone else and of moving rhythmically (this may need to be demonstrated). Make clear what needs to be done (books straightened up, materials or equipment replaced, or paper picked up and put in the trash can) and where it is to be placed, plus any other relevant instructions. Depending on what is to be done, it may be necessary to modify the words to fit the task. If this is the case, let students suggest relevant words.

3. After giving thorough directions as to what is to be accomplished, children move away from their desks and begin the "picking up" process (or other appropriate activity). Repeat the song until the task is accomplished.

Variation:

By changing the words it is possible to transform this song into a simple action song. Typical words may be:

> *Let's march along, let's march along,*
> *Let's march along in time.*
> *Let's march along, let's march along,*
> *Let's march along in time.*

Basic movements may be substituted: skip, hop, gallop, tiptoe, skate, with the accompanying appropriate activity as the song is sung. While no specific formation is required, it is better if children form a circle or a straight line so that the movement is done in the same direction and the children do not bump into each other.

II–14   SKIP, SKIP, SKIP   Grades K–3

A simple singing game in which one child chooses a basic movement for all others in the circle to do.

Objective: To practice fundamental or basic movements in a rhythmical manner.

Formation: Children form a circle in an open space area.

Skip, Skip, Skip

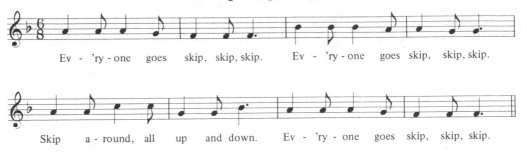

Ev - 'ry - one goes skip, skip, skip. Ev - 'ry - one goes skip, skip, skip.

Skip a - round, all up and down. Ev - 'ry - one goes skip, skip, skip.

Procedure:

1. Teach the song to the children.

2. Instruct children to form a circle in the open space area. Sing the song again and have everyone skip in a counterclockwise direction around the circle.

3. Choose one child to demonstrate another basic movement, such as hopping, marching, walking, running, sliding, galloping, tiptoeing, for the entire class to do. The words of the song will also need to be modified to include the chosen movement; for example, if the child chooses hopping, the children will all hop while they sing:

   Everyone goes hop, hop, hop.
   Everyone goes hop, hop, hop.
   Hop around, all up and down.
   Everyone goes hop, hop, hop.

   Other motions that are not locomotor may also be chosen, such as clapping or nodding.

4. The child who chose the motion just performed by the class then chooses another child who will name a motion for the class to sing and perform. The activity continues in this fashion for as long as the teacher wishes.

II–15   IF YOUR NAME BEGINS WITH
THE LETTER YOU HEAR   Grades K–3

Children whose names begin with a designated letter sound stand up and sing the second verse.

Objective: To discriminate the letter or sound with which their names (or other items) begin.

Formation: No specific formation is required.

If Your Name Begins with the Letter You Hear

1. If your name be - gins with the let - ter you hear, stand up, stand up. If your name be - gins with the let - ter you hear, stand up and take a bow. "B."*

Verse 2:

If my name begins with the letter you sound,
  I'll stand, I'll stand.
If my name begins with the letter you sound,
  I'll stand and take a bow.

Procedure:

1. Teach both verses of the song above.

2. This song may utilize the skill of letter recognition or sound (phonic) recognition. With younger children, you or the leader may wish to use the letter and would, therefore, sing "B" in the last measure. If the children are academically able to discriminate letters by sound, you or the leader will sing or say the sound of the letter selected. While the vowel sounds may be easily sung on a sustained pitch, this is not true of consonant sounds, which may have to be said instead of sung at the end of the first verse.

3. Before singing the first verse, instruct the students whose names begin with the letter sung or said at the end of the first verse to stand and sing the second verse and then to take a bow at the end. You then sing the first verse using any letter you wish at the end, and the appropriate students respond with the second verse.

4. You (or the leader) then repeat the first verse, using a different letter sound. Again, the students whose names begin with that sound stand to sing and take a bow.

5. The game continues in this fashion until you determine that it is over. After children learn the song well and understand how to play the game, you might choose various students to take turns as the leader to sing the first verse and give a letter sound.

Variation:

1. As mentioned in Procedure Step 2 above, instead of using letter sounds, you may wish to use the letters themselves. Depending upon the skill you wish to develop, sing the letter in the last measure after the first verse, or hold up a card with the letter printed on it (or write the letter on the blackboard).
2. Pass out pictures of well-known objects to each student before the game begins. After you sing or sound out the selected letter, each student who has a picture of an item that begins with that letter stands.

II–16   GUESS THE TUNE   Grades 1–4

Two or more familiar song titles are listed on the blackboard. The students try to guess which one is being clapped by the leader.

Objective: To discriminate which of two or more songs is being clapped.

Formation: No special formation is required.

Procedure:

1. On the blackboard, list the titles of two or more songs with which the students are familiar, and number each title. The number of songs may be reduced to two for younger children and increased to four for older or more capable children. Three such songs might be:
   A. "It's a Small World After All"
   B. "Yankee Doodle"
   C. "This Old Man"

2. Tell students you are going to clap the rhythm to one of the songs listed on the blackboard and that they are to listen and identify the song by holding up the appropriate number of fingers (one finger for "It's a Small World," two fingers for "Yankee Doodle," or three fingers for "This Old Man"). Do this three or four times, giving the correct answer immediately after they show the number of fingers indicating one of the songs listed.

3. After students understand what is expected of them and are familiar with the numbers of each song on the blackboard, ask them to close their eyes while you clap and have the students identify the song by holding up their fingers. It may be necessary to review the number of each song just before they close their eyes, and perhaps even after they close their eyes. The closed eyes are necessary to evaluate who can and cannot discriminate among the songs. Otherwise, students who cannot discriminate may find themselves looking at others' fingers to determine the answer. This type of evaluation also lets you know whether you need to decrease or increase the number of song titles and whether you need to select songs on your list that are very different or only slightly different.

4. Certain students may be selected to clap a song, and the rest of their classmates hold up the appropriate number of fingers.

II–17   WHOSE NAME?   Grades 1–4

The rhythms of children's names in the class are reviewed. The leader claps one name rhythm and all those children whose names fit the rhythm stand.

Objectives: To recognize your own name rhythm when it is clapped.
To clap name rhythms for others to identify.

Formation: No special formation is required.

Procedure:

1. Announce that everyone's name can be clapped with the hands. To illustrate, say and clap your name or some of the student's names. For example:

Mary

Harriet

Nathaniel

Dean

Elizabeth

Suzanne

2. After demonstrating two or more of the names represented in the classroom, ask volunteers to say and clap the rhythm of their own names. You may need to assist some of them. After the rhythm is established for each student's name, have everyone join in clapping and saying each one.

3. Tell the students that you are now going to clap one rhythm and that all students whose names fit that rhythm should stand immediately. Ask the class to help you check to see if all who should be standing are. Continue in this vein with other name rhythms.

Variation:

Give out rhythm instruments for students to tap out name rhythms as a follow-up activity for the plan above. After all students whose names fit the tapped-out rhythm have stood and been verified by you or the class, invite all students to tap out the rhythm just heard and chant one or more of the names that fit it.

II–18   TONE CALL GAME   Grades K–3

One student closes his eyes and tries to guess which student sings a tone call after the leader.

Objectives: To identify the person answering the leader's tone call.
To determine the direction from which the tone call came.

Formation: No special formation is required.

Tone Calls:

Hel - lo

Guess who — I am.

Procedure:

1. Tell students that you are going to play a singing game with them that requires them to listen very carefully. Before starting the game, sing one of the tone calls above and have the students sing it back right after you.

2. Ask one student to hide his eyes by putting his head down on the desk. Tell him to keep his head down until after the tone calls are sung. Sing one of the above tone calls and point to one of the other students to sing it back as a solo. At this point, the student whose head is down on the desk may look up and must identify the student who sang the call. If the singer is correctly identified, the singer then hides her eyes to guess who the next singer is to repeat the tone call after you. If the singer is not correctly identified by the one whose eyes were hidden, then he is given one additional chance to listen and guess. The guesser hides his eyes once again and the same person is asked to sing the tone call after you. If the singer is identified this time, then the game

goes on as outlined above (the singer becomes the new guesser, hiding her eyes). If the singer is not correctly identified, then the singer holds up his hand (praise the guesser if he has correctly identified the direction from which the sound came) to identify himself, and then becomes the new guesser.

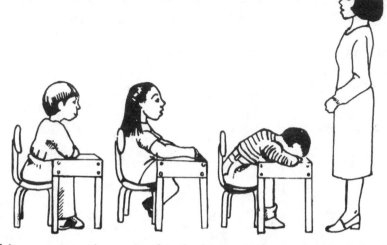

3. This game continues in this fashion until you decide it is time to stop.

Variation:

Instead of asking the student who guesses the singer of the tone call to hide his eyes on the desk, you might have him come to a designated wall or screen to hide his eyes so he will not have the advantage of his proximity or close distance to the singer as a clue. This way, the guesser is a distance away from all the other students.

II–19   TONE CALL GAME—
CONCEPT FORMATION   Grades K–3

Students are asked to respond to tone calls that require them to use concepts of color, shape, days of the week, and so on.

Objective: To discriminate colors, shapes, or other concepts.

Formation: No special formation is required.

Materials: Students are given colored construction paper cut into various shapes—circle, square, triangle, and rectangle.

Tone Calls:

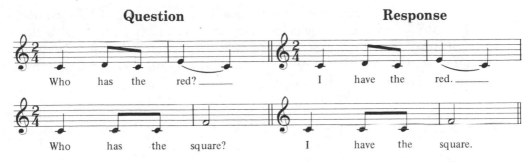

Procedure:

1. Prepare the various shapes ahead of time (circle, square, triangle, and rectangle). Cut them from construction paper of whatever colors you would like to review and/or teach. Suggested colors are yellow, red, blue, green, black, purple, orange, pink, and brown. Younger children would be given a smaller selection of colors (perhaps only three or four), where older or more advanced children would get a much wider selection. Hand out one colored shape to each student.

2. Tell students that you are going to sing them a question, such as, *Who has the red?* and that all students who have a shape that is colored red should hold it up (or stand) and sing the response, *I have the red.* Each time the students respond, check (with the help of the class) to see if all the reds responded. After students understand what to do, continue to sing the question, mixing up the colors, with the appropriate students responding immediately afterward.

3. When students become comfortable with the game and are able to check the answers quickly, instead of pausing between each question-response set, continue singing the next question without a pause or break in rhythm between the sets. This requires the students to stay alert and to respond rapidly.

4. If students are also somewhat familiar with shapes, change the question so that you are singing, *Who has the circle?* (square, triangle, rectangle). Practice these concepts for a few minutes.

5. When the students feel comfortable with Procedure Step 4, mix the color and shape questions and ask them to respond accordingly.

Variation:

Another concept that can be adapted to the tone call format is that of the days of the week, including the related terms of today, yesterday, and tomorrow. Below is a tone call that might be used; but keep in mind that any tune can be used and the wording can be changed according to your purpose.

II-20   FARMER   Grades K-3

Students sing about and imitate the various chores of a farmer.

Objective: To act out rhythmically various chores that a farmer might do.

Formation: No special formation is required though each student does need room to stand and do the various movements.

Farmer

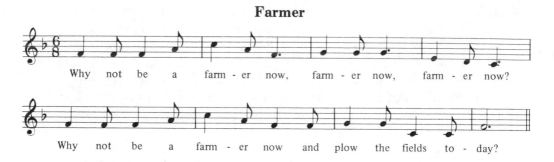

Verse 2:

*Here's the way we plow the field, plow the field plow the field.
Here's the way we plow the field so early Monday morning.*

Verse 3:

*Here's the way we plant the field, plant the field, plant the field.
Here's the way we plant the field so early Tuesday morning.*

Verse 4:

Here's the way we milk the cow . . . so early Wednesday morning.

Verse 5:

Here's the way we feed the stock . . . so early Thursday morning.

Verse 6:

Here's the way we gather eggs . . . so early Friday morning.

Verse 7:

Here's the way we cut the hay . . . so early Saturday morning.

Procedure:

1. Discuss some of the chores that have to be done on a farm. If students have trouble thinking of things, be ready to supply some answers. (See verses above.)

2. Use their words (make sure they fit the tune) or the words above, and have one or more students demonstrate an appropriate movement for each of the verses performed. After the class decides on a movement for each verse, sing the song and do the movements.

Variation:

For any occupation, students can compose words and movements that are appropriate. This is an excellent way to review the functions performed by community helpers.

II–21   ONE LITTLE SKELETON   Grades K–4

Children are chosen to portray various Halloween characters, that are featured in successive verses of the song.

Objectives: To dramatize various Halloween characters with rhythmic motions. To count from one to five.

Formation: From one to five students are called to the open space in front of the classroom to dramatize the various Halloween characters in each verse. In most cases, the characters will move around skipping, walking, and so on, in the front or among the other students in the classroom.

One Little Skeleton

One lit - tle skel - e - ton jump - ing up and down,

Jump-ing up and down, Jump-ing up and down. One lit - tle skel - e - ton

jump - ing up and down, For this is Hal - lo - ween.

Verse 2:

Two little witches flying through the air . . .

Verse 3:

Three little pumpkins walking in a row . . .

Verse 4:

Four little goblins skipping down the street . . .

Verse 5:

Five little children playing trick or treat . . .

Procedure:

1. Teach the first verse to the song above. It is simple enough, with its catchy tune and repetition of words, so that it can be learned rather quickly. Ask if anyone can demonstrate the way they think a skeleton might move.

   After one or more demonstrate typical movements, invite the entire group to move as a skeleton, using any of the movements demonstrated, or making up their own, while everyone sings the verse.

2. Teach the next verse, *Two little witches flying through the air.* Invite one or more students to come up and demonstrate movements and noises that such a character might make. Then ask the entire group to pretend to be witches while they sing the second verse.

3. Do the same as you did in verses one and two with the remaining three verses of the song.

4. Instead of inviting the entire group to dramatize each character, select individual children to portray the characters in each verse. For instance, one child would be selected to be the skeleton jumping up and down; two children would be selected to be the witches flying through the air. As each verse is sung by the group, the selected students come to the open area in front of the classroom to act out their parts.

Variation:

Guide children in making up their own verses relating to the Halloween holiday or any holiday. Other characters about which verses may be created for Halloween are black cats or ghosts. Children should also make appropriate movements for the verses or leave them to the interpretation of individuals. These verses may be performed in much the same way as outlined in Procedure Steps 1–4 above.

II–22   BARNACLE BILL   Grades K–4

One or more children bounce balls (or pretend to bounce balls) while the group sings.

Objective: To bounce a ball in rhythm to the song.

Formation: The students chosen to bounce the balls could come to the front of the classroom for all to see or, if there is a room, stand in front of their desks to bounce the balls.

Materials: One or more balls of any size. The younger the children, the larger the balls should be.

Barnacle Bill

1. When Bar - na - cle Bill was one ___ he learned to play the

drum. ___ Bon - nie o - ver in the clo - ver, Half past one. ___

Verse 2:

When Barnacle Bill was two he learned to buckle his shoe.
Bonnie over in the clover, Half past two.

Verse 3:

When Barnacle Bill was three he learned to climb a tree . . .

Verse 4:

When Barnacle Bill was four he learned to scrub the floor . . .

Verse 5:

When Barnacle Bill was five he learned to swim and dive . . .

Procedure:

1. Teach the song above, singing one or more verses.
2. Tell the students that you have a new way to keep time with the music and that you will demonstrate. Using a medium-sized ball, bounce it on the accent (beats one and four). Ask for a volunteer to come up and bounce the ball with you (using a second ball if another is available).

3. Ask several volunteers to come to the front of the classroom to bounce balls in time to the music while the class sings. The number of balls available is the limiting factor, but two to four should be available. It may be a good idea to encourage the other students (without balls) to pretend to bounce a ball in order to

practice before their turns. Each time a new verse is sung, a new set of bouncers should come to the front. Those students who are able to bounce the ball in time without missing or losing the ball are winners.

Variations:

1. Pair students off and have them bounce a ball to each other so that the ball is bounced on the accents throughout the song. Those partners who do not miss or lose the ball are winners.

2. Encourage students to vary the way in which they bounce the ball. One variation is to use alternate hands each time the ball is bounced. Others may wish to try and bounce it behind their backs, or in and out under their legs.

3. Invite the students to make up new stanzas to the song so that the last word of the first line rhymes with the number word, which is changed in each stanza.

4. As the different verses are sung, call for volunteers to set the clock face so that the time ("half past one") mentioned in the last line of the verse is shown. The verses can go all the way to twelve (provided the children make up that many verses in Variation 3).

II–23   THE ELEPHANT SONG   Grades K–4

The song begins with one child pretending to be an elephant. At the end of each verse, an additional elephant is chosen to "hook" on to the growing parade. On the last verse, the first elephant "weaves" a web by leading the line under the clasped hands of the others.

Objective: To move rhythmically while pretending to be elephants on parade.

Formation: From one to nine elephants join hands and march around an open classroom area pretending to be elephants on parade.

The Elephant Song

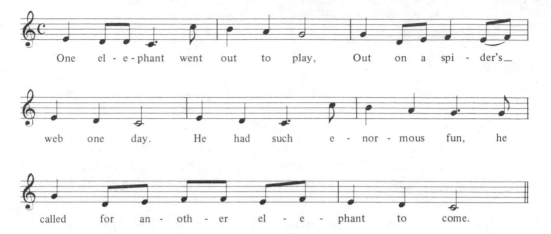

One el-e-phant went out to play, Out on a spi-der's
web one day. He had such e-nor-mous fun, he
called for an-oth-er el-e-phant to come.

Verse 2:

*Two elephants went out to play, Out on a spider's web one day.
They had such enormous fun, They called for another elephant to
come.*

Verses 3–9:

Three elephants . . .

Procedure:

1. Teach "The Elephant Song." (The activity can be done before the song is taught with you singing or a record playing the song.)

2. Ask several students to illustrate how an elephant moves while the class sings (or you sing) the song (or the record plays).

3. Let the class decide which movement they would like to adopt for the elephant line that is to be formed.

4. The student whose movement is chosen will be the leader of the elephant parade. He will need to place his left hand behind him for the next "elephant" (who is chosen by the first elephant on the last phrase of the first verse) to grasp with his right hand so that the effect is like elephants in a circus parade. The second elephant will then choose a third elephant on the last phrase of the second verse. This procedure continues until nine (or whatever number you desire) elephants form the parade.

5. On the last verse, *Nine elephants went out to play*, the lead elephant begins to weave in and out under the joined hands of the other elephants, creating a "spider's web." You may need to lead this activity the first time it is done.

Variation:

Lead students in a discussion concerning the meaning of the words in the song. For example, could an elephant really jump on a spider's web? If he could, what experience would this be similar to in real life for us? Who knows what "enormous" means?

II–24   WARMER OR COLDER?   Grades K–4

A child is expected to locate a designated person in the class through singing clues given by the group as they sing a familiar song. Louder singing means the child is getting closer to the target and softer singing means he is getting farther away.

Objective: To find a designated target (person) through clues given by singing volume.

Formation: Only one child needs to move about in this game. The child who is "It" goes to a remote place in the classroom or perhaps outside the door while the class selects the target (who is a designated person). When this has been accomplished, "It" is called back in the room, walking around at random while following the volume clues given in the singing. Any familiar song may be used.

Are You Sleeping?

Procedure:

1. Review the above song (or whatever familiar song you choose).

2. Tell the children that they are going to play a game using a song. Send one child outside the door or to a remote part of the room, where he hides his eyes. Select one child to be the "target" whom the other child (the one sent outside), hereinafter called "It," tries to identify. When "It" hears the class start singing, this is his signal to return to find the target. The initial singing should be fairly soft since "It" is far away from the target. "It" walks among his classmates, and as he comes closer to the child designated as the target, the singing gets louder and louder; the farther away "It" gets from the target, the softer the singing. "It" receives two chances to identify the target. As soon as the target is identified, "It" joins his classmates, and the identified target now becomes the new "It."

3. Continue the activity as long as you wish. The class may wish to change songs after singing one for a while.

Variations:

1. Reverse the clues so that loud singing indicates distance from the target and soft singing indicates proximity to the target.

2. Instead of appointing a child to be the target, select an inanimate object, or anything else, in the classroom.

II–25   FIVE LITTLE PUMPKINS   Grades K–4

Five students are selected to sing and act out the part of each pumpkin. The rest of the song is sung by the entire group.

Objectives: For selected individuals to sing a solo part expressively. To associate ordinal numbers with their relative cardinal numbers.

Formation: The five children chosen as soloists for the song may (but are not required to) come to the front of the classroom.

Five Little Pumpkins

From *Singing and Rhyming* of *Our Singing World* series,
© Copyright, 1958, 1957, 1950, by Ginn and Company
(Xerox Corporation). Used with permission.

Procedure:

1. Before asking the students to sing any part of this song, it is necessary for them to know it well. Therefore, it may be necessary to teach this song and review it several times before the following steps can be done.

2. While teaching and reviewing the song (before any soloists are selected), discuss how each of the lines would be sung by the five pumpkins. For instance, on the line sung by the first pumpkin, *Oh my, it's getting late*, it would be done with concern (somewhat as a little old lady might say it). The next solo line, *There are witches in the air!* would be sung as though the pumpkin were frightened. Encourage facial and body expression as well as expressive singing. While the class is learning the song, it might be advisable to assign the solo parts to different rows or tables in the classroom.

3. After students feel comfortable with the song, select five students to sing each of the pumpkins' lines as a solo. Make sure that the soloists are in order from left to right in front of the classroom. Review the ordinal positions of the soloists with the class. Direct the class in the parts they sing together and cue each soloist as it is her turn.

4. Change soloists and sing the song again.

Variations:

1. Instead of selecting soloists to sing the pumpkins' parts, have all the children sing the entire song and use the five fingers of one hand as though they were the five pumpkins. Each finger in turn should move appropriately as the different lines are sung. Review the ordinal positions of each of the fingers.

2. Choose five different instruments to do the solo parts of the five pumpkins. Each instrument will play the rhythm of the solo line it has been assigned.

II-26   COUNTING SONG   Grades K-4

Ten children are seated in chairs in front of the room with one additional child "falling out of bed" in each verse until there are none left.

Objective: To count backwards and forwards from one to ten while demonstrating the numbers with an activity.

Formation: Ten chairs should be placed in the front of the room. Students occupy all ten chairs on the first verse and gradually move over one chair to the right on each verse, routing one child out of his place. After the number of students reaches zero, the students begin returning, one at a time, on each verse.

Counting Song

Camp Song

1. There were ten in the bed and the lit-tle one said, "Roll o-ver, roll o-ver!" so they all rolled o-ver and one fell out.

Last stanza:

21. There were ten in the bed and the lit-tle one said, *"Good night."*

Verse 2:

There were nine in the bed . . .

Verses 3–9:

Decrease the number by one on each verse.

Verse 10:

There was one in the bed and the little one said,
  "Roll over, roll over!"
So they all rolled over and one fell out.

Verse 11:

There was none in the bed and the little one said,
  "Roll over, roll over!"
They all rolled over and one fell in.

Verses 12–21:

Increase the number by one each verse.

Procedure:

1. Teach the above song by singing a few (one to three) verses.

2. Set up ten chairs side by side in front of the classroom, and select ten children to occupy them. On *Roll over* all children move one seat to the right, and the one deprived of a seat steps aside. On verse 11, the process reverses with children moving one seat to the left as all the children return one by one. On verse 21 (the last one), all pretend to sleep and the last child whispers *good night.*

3. The entire class sings the song as the ten children go through the procedure outlined in step 2. If you wish, *Roll over, roll over* may be sung as a solo by the child who is about to "roll out of the bed" on each verse on the first ten, and by the child who is about to return on verses 12-20.

II-27   OCTI THE OCTOPUS   Grades K-4

Draw an octopus on the blackboard (or have a student draw an octopus). One student is asked to come to the blackboard armed with an eraser to erase a leg of the octopus each time the song says he loses one of them. The octopus ends up with no legs as the surprise ending of the song indicates.

Objective: To count in reverse order from eight to zero as a student gradually erases "legs" to coincide with the number sung in each verse.

Formation: One student will need to be at the blackboard armed with an eraser.

Octi the Octopus

Did you hear of Oct - i, the Oct - o - pus? He went down and he lost a leg. Then we could - n't call him an oct - o - pus, so we called him a sev - en - o - pus.

Verse 2:

Did you hear of Sevie, the Seven-o-pus?
He went down and he lost a leg.
Then we couldn't call him a seven-o-pus,
So we called him a six-o-pus.

Verse 3:

Did you hear of Sixy, the six-o-pus?
He went down and he lost a leg.
Then we couldn't call him a six-o-pus,
So we called him a five-o-pus.

Verse 4:

Did you hear of Fivey, the five-o-pus . . .
So we called him a four-o-pus.

Verse 5:

Did you hear of Foury, the four-o-pus . . .
So we called him a three-o-pus.

Verse 6:

Did you hear of Threey, the three-o-pus . . .
So we called him a two-o-pus.

Verse 7:

Did you hear of Twoey, the two-o-pus . . .
So we called him a one-o-pus.

Verse 8:

Did you hear of Oney, the one-o-pus . . .
So we called him a GREAT BIG BLOB!

Procedure:

1. Ask if anyone knows what an octopus is. After satisfactory answers have been given, review the fact that an octopus has eight legs (and perhaps that "octo" means eight).

2. Draw a rough outline of an octopus on the blackboard low enough for the children to reach it. Have the children count the number of legs to make sure there are eight.

3. Tell the children that you are going to sing them a song about an octopus who gets in trouble all the time. Invite them to join you in singing as soon as they can (the eight verses are very repetitive and, therefore, easy to learn). At the end of verse one, ask the children what they can do so that the drawing of the octopus

will look like the one in the song. (They should erase one leg.) Continue singing the successive verses and erasing an additional leg after each verse.

4. Now that the children have heard the song enough to sing it with you, sing the entire song over again. Call up one child to come to the blackboard and erase the legs of the new octopus, which you or a child will draw, one at a time.

5. If there is time, the children may wish to repeat the song again, but this time call several children to come to the blackboard. Have each child draw his own octopus (have the class check the number of legs on each one before beginning to sing). Each child will erase an additional leg on his octopus at the end of each verse.

II–28   A VALENTINE   Grades 1–4

Children are asked to make up their own words to the last phrase, which would be appropriate for a Valentine card and also fit the tune.

Objective: To compose a suitable line for a Valentine card which also fits the tune.

Formation: No special formation is required. Students would probably be more comfortable remaining seated while doing this activity.

A Valentine

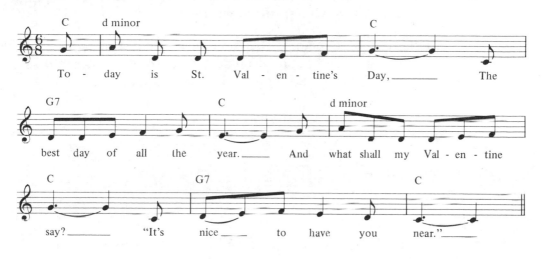

From *Growing with Music*, Book 2, Wilson et al. (Englewood
Cliffs, NJ, Prentice-Hall, Inc., 1970)

Procedure:

1. Teach the above song.
2. Call the students' attention to the last phrase of the song, *It's
   nice to have you near*, and tell them that this is a phrase that
   would be appropriate to include on a Valentine's Day card that
   you might make yourself and send to a friend. Invite students to
   make up other phrases that also would be appropriate for a Valentine's Day card and that would fit the end of this song (to substitute for the last phrase). It would be helpful to demonstrate
   by giving one or more examples, such as:

   > *Your voice is nice to hear.*
   > *I need you to talk with me.*
   > *Your smile is always dear.*

3. Write some of the suggested phrases on a piece of chart paper or
   the blackboard. Sing the song several times, substituting in a
   selected phrase from the chart or board each time.

II–29   HALLELU   Grades 2–6

Half the group sings *Hallelu* and the other half sings *Praise ye
the Lord*. The group singing must stand each time and then sit when
the other group sings.

Objective: To coordinate the standing position with the singing and the seated position with silence.

Formation: Everyone begins the song seated in their desks or chairs. There should be sufficient room for a rapid exchange of standing and sitting positions.

Hallelu

Procedure:

1. Teach the above song so that the group feels comfortable with it.

2. Divide the group into halves and assign one-half to sing *Hallelu* and the other side to sing *Praise ye the Lord*. Practice this singing arrangement once or twice. Next, instruct each half to stand when they sing their part and to immediately sit while the other half stands and sings. It is helpful if you direct each group when to stand and sit. The most likely place for the group to make an error is in the ninth measure. Through the eighth measure the groups alternate standing and sitting; this pattern changes in the ninth measure, where *Praise ye the Lord* is sung for the second time without the intervening *Hallelu*.

3. After each side feels comfortable with its part, have them trade parts so that the side formerly singing *Hallelu* is now singing *Praise ye the Lord!* and vice versa.

4. You might also divide the group into boys and girls.

II–30 SILENT SINGING Grades 2–6

While singing any familiar song, the group must follow the leader's signals to sing "silently" (just think the tune) or to sing so others can hear. These signals may be given several times during a song.

Objective: To retain pitch and rhythm even though the singing is not always audible.

Formation: No special formation is required. Students can do this activity seated.

Music: Any song that is known well by the students may be used in this activity. Suggested songs are:
"Yankee Doodle Went to Town"
"America"
"Rudolph the Red-Nosed Reindeer"
"Let There Be Peace on Earth"
"America the Beautiful"
"Rock-a-My Soul in the Bosom of Abraham"

Procedure:

1. Select any song that is well-known to the group and sing it through at least once.

2. Tell the group that they are going to sing the song through several times (until you stop them or until they sing it through a specified number of times). They are to begin singing it audibly and continue to do so until you give them the signal to sing it silently or in their minds only. (Any signal may be used: you could put your index finger to your closed lips, or use one finger to indicate silent singing and two fingers to indicate audible singing.) At the signal they are to immediately stop singing and just think the tune. At a later point, give the signal (palms up or two fingers raised) to begin singing aloud again. You can give these signals as often as you choose. The trick is for everyone to begin singing at the same point on the same pitch.

II–31   ECHO CLAPPING   Grades K–6

The leader claps a rhythm and the group imitates it.

Objective: To repeat a leader's rhythm exactly as it was given.

Formation: No special formation is required. Students can comfortably do this activity while seated.

Procedure:

1. Tell students that you are going to clap different rhythms and that they are to listen carefully so they will be able to clap them immediately after you do. Demonstrate by clapping the following rhythm and having them repeat it immediately afterward:

It may be necessary to rehearse this with the group several times.

2. After they understand what is expected, continue doing the exercise without any pause unless they miss one. For instance,

Director   **Group Response**

As long as the group does a good job of repeating the rhythms, there is no need to pause. The last note of exercise 1 is a half note and is held two beats. Immediately after the two beats, the group should start their response on the next beat (which is the first beat of the very next measure). If the group's response is satisfactory, continue immediately with the next exercise (2) after waiting for the group's last note to be held two beats. If you or the group finds this method of operating too taxing, you might want to pause between the exercises.

3. You should feel free to make up as many exercises of whatever length and difficulty you choose. Students might also be called upon to be the director who claps rhythms for others to imitate.

4. If a rhythm is missed, ask the group to listen carefully as you clap it again and then try it a second time.

II–32   I WISH I HAD A NICKEL   Grades 2–5

Students pair off to sing this song and perform the clap-slap activity.

Objective: To move the hands rhythmically in coordination with a partner.

Formation: Students pair off and stand facing each other. If there is an odd number of students in the group, you will have to join the activity.

I Wish I Had a Nickel

I wish I had a nick - el, I wish I had a dime,

I wish I had a boy - friend that kissed me all the time.

Procedure:

1. Teach the above song, so that the students know it well.

2. Select a student who has good rhythm to come to the front of the classroom to help you demonstrate the little game that is played as you sing the song. The student faces you as you do the following movements:

With the open palm of the right hand, lightly tap the open palm of the right hand of the person facing you. The first tap will occur on the word *wish* (first full beat of the song).

On the second beat of the measure, each person claps his own two hands together.

On the first beat of the second measure, each person extends the left hand with open palms and taps the left hand of the other person.

On the second beat of the second measure, each person claps his own two hands together.

The above sequence continues throughout the entire song. It is extremely important to have the right hands of each person tap together on the first beat of the first full measure. Generally, if they start off correctly, the rest follows naturally.

3. After demonstrating the above movements while singing with one other student, ask the students to pair off and try the cooperative activity. It may be necessary to go very slowly through the movements without the singing at first, and then fit the movements to the song.

4. After students feel comfortable with the game, purposely challenge the students by speeding up the tempo. Have partners volunteer to come up and demonstrate their prowess.

II–33   JUMP DOWN, TURN AROUND   Grades 2–6

Several children are called to the front to do appropriate movements while others sing and clap the beat or accent.

Objective: To move rhythmically to the music while illustrating the meaning of the words.

Formation: From two to fifteen children may be called to the front of the room to do the indicated movements. These children may stand in one or two straight lines facing the remainder of the group, who are in their seats singing.

Jump Down, Turn Around

Oh, jump down, turn a-round, pick a bale of cot-ton. Jump down, turn a-round, pick a bale a day. Oh, Man-dy, pick a bale of cot-ton. Oh, Man-dy, pick a bale a day.

Procedure:

1. Teach the above song to the group.

2. Discuss the meaning of the words with the group. What is occurring? (picking cotton) What is the setting? (probably a large cotton plantation) How is cotton picked? (by bending down to pull the cotton off a low plant)

3. Guide the students as they decide what movements should be done throughout the song. In many cases, the words will indicate the movement, but it is important they do the movements with decided rhythm and gusto.

4. Select several students to come to the front of the class to perform the movements that the group decided upon in step 3, as the rest of the group sing from their seats. The song may be sung several times, changing the performers of the movements each time.

5. Rhythm instruments may be used by some children as the group sings and some students perform the movements. Encourage students to experiment with the rhythm instruments until they hear something they like.

II-34   I AM A MUSICIAN   Grades 2-6

Students take turns doing the leader's part, which involves singing a solo on the part of the verse identifying the instrument of the band or orchestra which is featured. Select an illustrative playing motion for that instrument, which the group imitates, as all sing the instrument part.

Objective: To identify by name various instruments of the band or orchestra and develop a representative playing motion for each.

Formation: One student comes to the front of the group and selects an instrument of the band or orchestra which he will pretend to play during the refrain. All other students remain seated.

I Am a Musician

Origin unknown

Leader: I am a musician, I can ____ play ____

Group: What can you play? ____ Leader: I play the bass viol.

Refrain:

Leader: Zum - ba, zum - ba, zum - ba, zum.   Zum - ba, zum - ba, zum - ba, zum.

Zum - ba, zum - ba, zum - ba, zum.   Zum - ba, zum - ba, zum.
(Pretend to play the bass viol.)

Verse 2:

Leader: *I am a musician, I can play.*
Group: *What can you play?*
Leader: *I play the piccolo.*
(Whistle above tune starting with the refrain.)

Verse 3:

Violin (vee-o, vee-o, vee-o la).
(Pretend to play a violin.)

Verse 4:

Bass drum (boomba, boomba,)
(Pretend to play a bass drum.)

Verse 5:

Cymbals (Zimba, zimba, zimba, zimba)
(Pretend to play cymbals.)

Verse 6:

Trumpet (ta ta ta ta, etc.)
(Pretend to hold and play the trumpet.)

Verse 7:

"I am the leader." (Piano plays or group sings "la" on refrain.)
(Students can conduct a two-or four-beat pattern.)

Procedure:

1. Teach one or two verses of the above song.

2. After students learn the song, demonstrate the dialogue characteristic of the song by singing the leader's part yourself and asking the class to sing the group part. If this is a problem, the class
   can be divided into two parts with one half singing the leader's
   part and the other half singing the group's part.

3. Identify some of the instruments in the band or orchestra and
   typical holding positions and playing motions. The instruments
   mentioned in verses one through six may be used exclusively or
   others may be mentioned and added or substituted for the above
   verses.

4. Call for a volunteer to select an instrument and sing the leader's
   part while the remainder of the class sings the group's part. The
   entire group sings and does the motion on the refrain, though it is
   the leader's responsibility determine the motion and initiate it.

5. Change leaders and instruments for successive verses until the
   allotted time has elapsed or until you decide it is time to change
   activities.

6. On verse 7, you may find it necessary to give some basic instruc-
   tion in conducting a two- or four-beat pattern before a student is
   selected as the leader for that verse.

II–35   THE DEATH OF MR. FLY   Grades 2–5

Children dramatize the words of this song.

Objective: To interpret the words of the song through dramatization.

Formation: The characters in the dramatization will need to come to
the front in an open classroom area.

The Death of Mr. Fly

Mis - ter Fly climbed up a tree, Cried, "I'm high as high can be!"

Lost his grip, came crash-ing down, Smashed to pie - ces on the ground.

From *Silver Burdett Music I* © 1981 Silver Burdett Company.
Reprinted by permission.

Verse 2:

When the insects heard the sound
Echoing for miles around,
They began to buzz and cry,
"Quick! First aid for Mister Fly!"

Verse 3:

"Where's a bandage?" "Where's a splint?"
"Get some liniment and lint!"
"Someone give him aspirin!"
"Should we call the doctor in?"

Verse 4:

Then a wise old flea spoke out,
"You don't know what you're about!
He's beyond the reach of aid,
Get a pick and get a spade!"

Verse 5:

Then at last those insects knew
What they really had to do!
Now his tombstone bears the scrawl:
"He who climbs too high must fall."

Procedure:

1. Teach the first verse of the song above. Special attention may
   need to be given to the sixth measure, in which the last note
   ("D" on the word *down*) goes a little lower than most singers ex-
   pect. After the group sings the first verse satisfactorily, sing the
   other four verses.

2. Discuss what is happening in the story told by all five verses. Review the words if necessary.

3. Invite different students to demonstrate how the different parts should be sung (the type of expression) and what movements would be appropriate.

4. Tell students that they are going to act out the song while the class sings it. Have the students read the words of the song and decide how many characters should be cast. You or the group can decide on the number of characters; a recommended number is six—the fly, four insects (to sing one line apiece of verse three), and the flea, who sings in verse 4.

5. Cast the characters, making sure they know what parts they are to sing.

   Verse 1: Everyone sings this verse except for the words *"I'm as high as high can be!"* which are sung by the fly.

   Verse 2: Everyone but the fly and the flea sings verse 2, except for the last line *"Quick! First aid for Mister Fly!"* This line is sung by the four insects who have solo lines in verse 3.

   Verse 3: Each of the four insects will pick one line to sing as a solo.

   Verse 4: Everyone sings the first line of verse 4, and the flea sings the rest.

   Verse 5: Everyone sings the last verse.

6. Give help with expression and the staging, where needed.

7. If there is time, change the cast of characters and perform the entire song again.

II–36   BEAR HUNT   Grades 2–6

The leader tells a story about going on a bear hunt and uses his hands in such a manner as to suggest the various motions of walking, running, climbing, swimming, and so on, of the hunter. When the hunter encounters the bear, he turns and runs, so that the prior motions are all done in a rapid reverse order. The children do the motions with the leader throughout the story.

Objectives: To listen carefully in order to do the suggested appropriate motions to certain action words. To do the accumulated motions in reverse order at a rapid pace.

Formation: The children may remain seated at their desks while participating in this game.

Procedure:

1. Tell the children that they are going on a bear hunt with you today and that it is important that they do all the motions with you. Instruct them to place their hands on their desks initially and to listen carefully and watch you (the leader) for the right motions at the right time.

2. Below is the script that you follow (it is suggested that the script be practiced several times before doing it with the group so that the sequence and words can be said without too much reliance upon the written copy). On the right are the hand motions that you and the students are to do at designated points.

THE BEAR HUNT

Look at that tall grass!	Do a walking pattern
Can't go around.	by alternately moving
Can't go under.	hands on desk.
Let's go through.	
(Pause while brushing	Brush palms of hands
palms of hands a few	together back and forth.
times.)	
I see a huge lake.	(Continue to brush
Can't go around.	palms together.)
Can't go under.	
Let's swim across.	Move arms in a swimming
	motion.
Scared?	(Continue with swimming
Not much.	motions and shake head in
	"No" response.)
I see a big-g-g tree.	(Continue swimming motion.)
Can't go around,	
Can't go under.	
Let's climb up.	Pretend to climb a tree by
	alternately putting one hand
	above the other.

I don't see any bears!	(Continue climbing motion and shake head "No.")
I see a bridge. Can't go around. Can't go under. Let's go over.	Do a walking pattern with hands.
I see a cave. Can't go around. Can't go over.	Gradually slow the walking pattern
Let's go through.	(Begin to whisper.)
I see two eyes.	Reach out as though to touch.
I see a nose. It's a bear!	(Shout this last line.)

Rapidly reverse all previous hand and arm motions as though running back from where you started. The reverse motions are as follows: walking, climbing, swimming, brushing palms together, and walking.

3. The students may wish to go through the entire activity again. If so, it might be wise to review the sequence of the rapid reverse motions and rehearse them once or twice before repeating everything. Emphasize that students should listen carefully and change to the designated motions immediately upon cue.

II–37   OLD WOMAN   Grades 3–6

Two students dramatize the text of the song, which may be sung as solos by the actors or by the entire group.

Objective: To dramatize the song as it is sung.

Formation: One boy and one girl will need to come to the front of the group in an open space area. The remainder of the group may remain in their seats.

Old Woman

Boy: Old wom - an, Old wom - an, Are you fond of card - ing?

Girl: Speak a lit - tle loud - er, sir, I'm ver - y hard of hear - ing.

Verse 2:

Old woman, old woman, are you fond of spinning?
Old woman, old woman, are you fond of spinning?
Speak a little louder, sir, I'm very hard of hearing.

Verse 3:

Old woman, old woman, will you darn my stocking?

Verse 4:

Old woman, old woman, will you let me court you?
Old woman, old woman, will you let me court you?
Speak a little louder, sir! I just begin to hear you.

Verse 5:

Old woman, old woman, don't you want to marry me.
Old woman, old woman, don't you want to marry me.
Oh, my goodness gracious me! I hear you now quite clearly.

Procedure:

1. Teach the above song, singing all five verses.

2. Discuss what is happening in the song. Point out that the man is trying to get the woman to do some of his chores for him and the woman feigns deafness as she does not want to do them. Convinced that the old woman is hard of hearing, he teases her by whispering the first part of the last two verses. The man's joke backfires as he finds out that the old woman is quite capable of hearing whatever she wants to hear.

3. Discuss movements and expressions that might be employed to dramatize the words of the song. Have several pairs of students act out the parts and let the class decide what parts of each dramatization they like best.

4. Appoint two persons to dramatize the song as it is sung by the group. Some of the actors may prefer to sing their parts as solos.

II–38 THERE WAS AN OLD WOMAN
WHO SWALLOWED A FLY   Grades 3–6

One or more students can dramatize the words. There may be a different student playing the old woman each time she swallows a different animal, or only one may do it.

Objective: To recall the cumulative sequence of animals as the song progresses.

Formation: Only those students called upon to play the old woman each time she swallows an animal will be in the open area in front of the group.

There Was an Old Woman Who Swallowed a Fly

American Folk Song

Verse 4:

There was an old woman who swallowed a cat;
Imagine that! To swallow a cat.
She swallowed a cat to swallow a bird to swallow a spider to swallow
  a fly,
And I don't know why she swallowed a fly.
Perhaps she'll die.

Verse 5:

There was an old woman who swallowed a dog.
What a hog to swallow a dog!
She swallowed a dog to swallow a cat to swallow a bird to swallow a
  spider to swallow a fly,
And I don't know why she swallowed a fly,
Perhaps she'll die.

Verse 6:

There was an old woman who swallowed a goat,
Just opened her throat and swallowed a goat.
She swallowed a goat to swallow a dog to swallow a cat to swallow
  a bird to swallow a spider to swallow a fly,
And I don't know why she swallowed a fly,
Perhaps she'll die.

Verse 7:

There was an old woman who swallowed a cow;
I don't know how she swallowed a cow.
She swallowed a cow to swallow a goat to swallow a dog to swallow
  a cat to swallow a bird to swallow a spider to swallow a fly,
And I don't know why she swallowed that fly,
Perhaps she'll die.

Verse 8:

(See below.)

8. There was an old wom-an who swal-lowed a horse, she's dead, of course!

Procedure:

1. Sing the entire song through so that the group hears the sequence in all eight verses. Teach the group the song.

2. After they have learned the song, appoint a different child to
   dramatize the new portion of each verse; one child will dramatize
   the old woman who swallowed a fly; a second child the old
   woman as she swallows the spider who wiggled and jiggled and

tickled inside her; a third child the old woman who swallows a bird; a fourth child the old woman who swallows a dog; and so on, so that each verse is covered by a different actor. After a new actor appears for the first time in each verse, she continues to play the part each time the assigned character is mentioned in the cumulative part of subsequent verses. Each child should decide upon some type of action or expression to use for the assigned character part.

II–39 THERE'S A HOLE IN THE BUCKET Grades 3–6

This song tells a story in its many verses, which may be dramatized by two students while the group sings.

Objective: To dramatize the story told in the verses of the song, which the group sings.

Formation: Two students come to the front of the group for the purpose of dramatizing the story. The group may remain in their seats as they sing.

There's a Hole in the Bucket

George: 1. There's a hole in the buck - et, dear Li - za, dear Li - za,
Liza: Mend the hole then, dear Geor - gie, dear Geor - gie, dear Geor - gie,

There's a hole in the buck - et, dear Li - za, a hole.
Mend the hole then, dear Geor - gie, dear Geor - gie, the hole.

Verse 2:

Georgie: *With what shall I mend it,*
Liza: *With a straw, then.*

Verse 3:

Georgie: *If the straw be too long, then,*
Liza: *Cut the straw, then,*

Verse 4:

Georgie: *With what shall I cut it,*
Liza: *With a knife, then,*

Verse 5:

Georgie: *If the knife be too dull, then,*
Liza: *Whet the knife, then,*

Verse 6:

Georgie: *With what shall I whet it,*
Liza: *With a stone, then,*

Verse 7:

Georgie: *If the stone be too rough, then,*
Liza: *Smooth the stone, then,*

Verse 8:

Georgie: *With what shall I smooth it,*
Liza: *With water,*

Verse 9:

Georgie: *In what shall I fetch it,*
Liza: *In a bucket,*

(Spoken) Georgie: **There's a hole in the bucket!**

Procedure:

1. Give each student a copy of the words to the song or place them on the blackboard or chart paper so that all can see them. Sing the first two or three verses to the students so that they hear the tune, and then ask them to join you in singing the rest of the verses.

2. After the entire song has been sung, ask students for an interpretation of what is happening in the song. Explain that the entire song is a dialogue between Georgie and Liza and that a logical sequence is involved in the many verses. This sequence should be helpful in cuing each successive verse.

3. Ask several students to demonstrate singing and acting out one or two of the verses. If you wish, the group might discuss which of the demonstrations expressed the meaning of the words well. The purpose here is not to select the best demonstration, but to emphasize those desirable aspects from each demonstration, if possible. For example, Jack pronounced his words clearly, Sue had good facial expression.

4. After pointing out some of the desirable qualities for acting out the words of the song (from step 3), select a boy and a girl to act out the roles of Georgie and Liza. In some cases, the actors may

wish to sing the parts as solos, and in other cases, the group may sing (boys sing Georgie's part and girls sing Liza's part) as the two students act out the parts.

5. If there is time, change actors and do the activity again.

II–40   DAISY (BICYCLE BUILT FOR TWO)   Grades 4–6

Two students, a boy and a girl, dramatize the verses as the group sings.

Objective: To dramatize the words of the song as it is sung by the group.

Formation: Only the two students involved in the dramatization will need to be out of their seats and in an open space area.

Daisy (Bicycle Built for Two)   Harry D'Acre

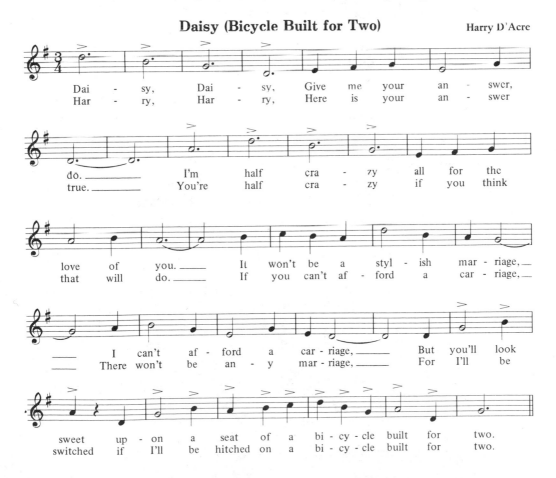

Dai - sy, Dai - sy, Give me your an - swer,
Har - ry, Har - ry, Here is your an - swer

do. _____ I'm half cra - zy all for the
true. _____ You're half cra - zy if you think

love of you. _____ It won't be a styl - ish mar - riage, __
that will do. _____ If you can't af - ford a car - riage, __

_____ I can't af - ford a car - riage, _____ But you'll look
_____ There won't be an - y mar - riage, _____ For I'll be

sweet up - on a seat of a bi - cy - cle built for two.
switched if I'll be hitched on a bi - cy - cle built for two.

Procedure:

1. Teach or review both verses of the above song.

2. Discuss the meaning of the words.

3. Ask for volunteers, a boy and a girl, to act out the words of the song as the group sings. The boys should sing the first verse as the boy dramatizes the words. The girls should sing the second verse as the girl dramatizes the words. If desired, elicit suggestions from the group for dramatizing the two verses.

4. Change actors and do the song again. Some of the actors may also feel comfortable singing the verses as solos.

II–41   THE COOKIE JAR GAME   Grades 3–6

The entire group engages in slap-clap movement, while a rhythmic question-response (solo and group) takes place. Any soloist missing the rhythm is automatically out.

Objective: To keep rhythm with the hands and voices while playing "The Cookie Jar Game."

Formation: Students could remain seated in their seats, but it is better if all participants form a circle either on the floor or with chairs.

Rhyme: "The Cookie Jar Game"
In this rhyme, the motions of alternately slapping and clapping the hands are as important as the rhyme. An "X" over a word indicates a clapping motion and an "O" indicates a slapping motion. The rhyme is said responsively by groups or individuals (one group or individual speaks and another replies). The number 1 indicates one group or individual and the number 2 indicates the other group or individual.

```
              o    x      o    x      o  x  o  x
All: Who stole the cookie from the cookie jar?—

                  o      x      o    x      o  x o
1: (The boys) stole the cookie from the cookie jar.
   (girls)
   (Kate)
   (Bob)
```

      x o   **x o**
2: Who me?   1: Yes, you!

      x o   **x o x**
2: Not me!   1: Then who?—

           o   x   o   x   o x o
2: *(The girls)* stole the cookie from the cookie jar.
     (boys)
     (Bob)
     (Kate)

At this point, if the rhyme is to be continued, the group or individual would go back to the third line (2) and keep repeating these three lines until all have had a chance to be accused or the group decides to stop. Different names should be substituted in the blanks so that someone new answers for number 2 each time.

Procedure:

1. Write the above rhyme on the blackboard or on chart paper.

2. Let the entire group practice saying the rhyme and doing the motions (do not divide into groups for this initial practice) until they feel comfortable with it.

3. Divide the group into two parts, boys and girls, and assign part 1 to the girls and part 2 to the boys. Everyone says the first line; then they divide into two groups. In the last line (group 2) the boys accuse the girls. At this point, everyone goes back to line three. The girls become group 2 saying, "Who me?" and the boys become group 1 saying, "Yes, you!" For example:

All: Who stole the cookie from the cookie jar?
Girls: The boys stole the cookie from the cookie jar.
Boys: Who, us?
Girls: Yes, you!
Boys: Not us!
Girls: Then who?
Boys: The girls stole the cookie from the cookie jar.
Girls: Who, us?
Boys: Yes, you!
Girls: Not us!
Boys: Then who?
Girls: The boys stole the cookie from the cookie jar.
(Continue by going back to the third line.)

4. After the above practice, the class should be fairly comfortable with the rhyme and motions and their use in a responsive setting. If not, it may be advisable to practice steps 1 and 2 more before trying the next activity.

This time, individual names of students in the class are used. Everyone says the first line, and a preselected person says the second line, using a student's name of his choosing (you, as the teacher, may need to say this line the first time). The accused person responds with "Who me?" The person who said the second line responds, "Yes, you!"

5. Students may be asked to stand by their desks or in a circle until they miss the hand or voice rhythm when they are accused. If they do miss the rhythm, they must sit down or leave the circle.

II–42   NANI WALE NA HALA
(PUILI STICK GAME)   Grades 4–6

Each student has two puili sticks and does various rhythmic movements by himself or with a partner.

Objective: To move the sticks in a prescribed order in rhythm to the music.

Formation: Participating students should be seated on the floor in whatever formation is deemed suitable. A circle or straight lines would be fine.

Nani Wale Na Hala

Hawaiian Folk Song
English Version by Alice Firgau

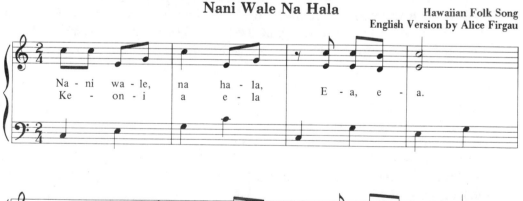

Equipment: Authentic puili sticks are best for this activity, but makeshift puili sticks can be made by rolling several thicknesses of heavy paper, tying the roll so it will stay, and cutting one end into narrow strips. If bamboo is available, it can be cut into lengths of twelve to eighteen inches and fringed at one end. A pair of these sticks will be needed by each participant.

Stick Movements:

The following are suggested patterns that may be used with the music. After the students are familiar with these, they may wish to make up their own patterns.

Pattern A:

Verse 1:

Measures 1–2 (one beat per movement):

Tap sticks together in front (about chest level).

Tap each stick on the floor on its respective side (right stick on right side and left stick on left side).

Tap sticks together in front of body (about chest level).

Tap each stick on the floor on its respective side.

Measures 3–4: Repeat steps for measures 1–2.

Measures 5–6:

Tap sticks together above the head.

Tap right stick on right shoulder.

Tap sticks together above the head.
Tap left stick on left shoulder.

Measures 7–8: Repeat steps for measures 5–6.

Verse 2:

Measures 1–4:

Tap crossed sticks overhead from right to left four beats.
Tap crossed sticks overhead from left to right four beats.

Measures 5–6:

Tap sticks overhead one beat.
Tap right shoulder with right stick.
Tap sticks overhead one beat.
Tap left shoulder with left stick.

Measures 7–8: Repeat steps for measures 5–6.

Alternate patterns that may be used are as follows:

Tap left shoulder with right stick.
Tap sticks on floor.
Tap right shoulder with left stick.
Tap sticks on floor.

Tap sticks on floor.
Partners tap right sticks together.
Tap sticks on floor.
Partners tap left sticks together.

Procedure:

1. Teach the above song.

2. A pair of puili sticks is needed for each participant. Rulers or implements made according to the directions above may be used instead.

3. Demonstrate one or more of the patterns described above. Each movement is done on the beat. After practice in manipulating the sticks in various patterns, teach a sequence of movements suggested above for the two verses of the song. Do the movements with the music.

4. After students are able to do the suggested movements with the song, some of them may wish to create new movements and sequences of movements.

II–43   TINIKLING (POLE DANCE)   Grades 4–6

One student at a time weaves his dance steps between and around two long poles manipulated by two other students.

Objective: To move in the appointed manner in conjunction with the movement of the two long poles.

Formation: As many sets of this game may be formed to operate simultaneously as there are equipment and space available. A set includes two students to manipulate the poles and one or two students to move around the poles.

Tinikling

English Words by Margaret Marks
Arranged by James Harris

Philippine Dance Song
Collected by Francisco Reyes Aguina

Ev-'ry-bod-y dance like the bird Tin - i - kling,
fast - er and fast - er, — don't stop,

As — he — jumps in and out, out — and in,
Left, — right, — left, right, you stop and — you hop,

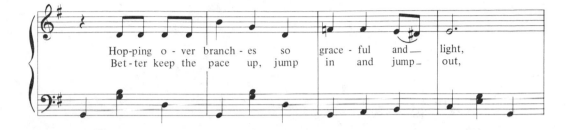

Hop-ping o-ver branch-es so grace-ful and light,
Bet-ter keep the pace up, jump in and jump out,

Keep in step and you'll dance this dance right,
Or the bam-boo will get you, watch

Now the dance goes out. Care-ful that the

clip and the clap of the bam-boo Come be-tween the

tip - ping, tap - ping toes! Care - ful when the
May - be there are

poles came to - geth - er, clip — clap, that — your —
some who can still jump and — hop, but — you —

feet are not caught in their — trap! Care - ful that the
can - not be blamed if you — stop!

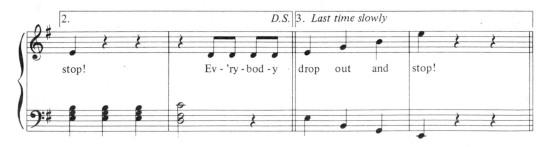

stop! Ev - 'ry - bod - y drop out and stop!

Equipment needed: Two bamboo poles six to nine feet long; two pieces of board thirty inches long and two inches thick.

Position: Set poles side by side about twelve inches apart
resting on pieces of wood, with a player at each
end, seated on the floor holding the ends of the
poles, as shown:

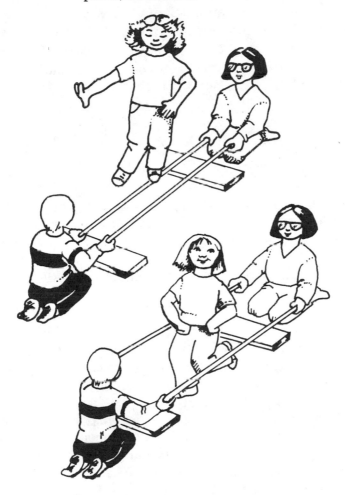

The players slide the poles together on the first beat
of each measure, then hit the boards on which they
rest on the second and third beats of each measure.

1   **2**   **3**

Hit poles   strike poles on boards
together

Basic Dance Step: stand outside the pole so that the poles are to the
dancer's right.

Measure 1: on beat 1, hop on left foot OUTSIDE the left pole;
            on beat 2, hop on right foot BETWEEN the poles;
            on beat 3, hop on left foot BETWEEN the poles.
Measure 2: on beat 1 hop on right foot OUTSIDE the right pole;
            on beat 2, hop on left foot BETWEEN the poles;
            on beat 3, hop on right foot BETWEEN the poles.

Continue throughout the song, alternating right and left sides. Dancers should always plan to have both feet outside the poles on the first beat of each measure, for that is when the poles click together.

From *Making Music Your Own*, Book 6, © 1971 Silver Burdett Company. Reprinted by permission.

Procedure:

1. If you wish, you may teach the song to the group so that they can sing it as the dance is done by various class members. However, the song can be taped by a pianist for use by the group whenever they perform it. The group may be interested to know that the game or dance is an imitation of the tinikling bird in the Philippines as he walks through the long stem grasses and over fallen tree limbs.

2. Before doing the dance, teach several students how to manipulate the poles. The two wooden boards (about thirty inches long and two inches thick) are set about five to nine feet apart and are used to rest the two six- to nine-foot long poles. The two long poles should be placed about twelve inches apart initially. A player is placed at each end to hold the two poles and manipulate them. On the first beat of each three-beat measure, they click the two poles together. On beats two and three, they pull the poles apart about twelve inches and strike the poles on the board. This is repeated throughout the dance.

3. Demonstrate the dancer's movement. The dancer should start on the left side of the pole and follow the steps outlined above. Practice without the music at first, and then with the music.

4. One dancer may participate per set of poles, or two dancers may participate at the same time. In the latter case, one dancer stands in back of the other during Part A (the first half of the song); In Part B, partners may stand across from each other, facing, so that the poles are to each dancer's left. As the Tinikling step is danced, the partners move toward each other and change sides with each measure of the music.

III

DANCE GAMES
AND ACTIVITIES
FOR LARGE GROUPS

This part is designed for those of you who must accommodate large groups with dance games and activities. It includes singing games, folk dances, and semi-modern social dance activities that can be used with groups of five or six and larger. The group size is limited only by the size of the open space area. Special formations, such as circles, reels, and squares, are characteristic of most of the activities.

More time is generally required to perform these activities, as many of the games and activities involve rules and a series of steps. If participants are unfamiliar with them, they need to be explained and taught. Even when they are familiar with the activities, managing large groups can still be time-consuming. A minimum time slot of ten to twenty minutes, depending upon the difficulty of the activity and the group's familiarity with it, is recommended. For some of the activities, a longer time period may be needed.

A problem frequently encountered with elementary children is that of pairing off with the opposite sex when participating in games and dances. Many of the boys and, occasionally, some of the girls object to having a partner of the opposite sex. That problem may need to be faced in some of the activities in this part calling for partners. A discussion prior to the activity, on considering the feelings of others when pairing off, could be helpful. If partner games and dances are often used, a rotation system in which partners are changed frequently and systematically is recommended. This way, any feelings of discomfort about being paired with a certain person may be alleviated by the fact that the assignment is of short duration. You may need to remind students of their manners and consideration for the feelings of others periodically before they engage in the activities.

Another way of dealing with the problem of partners is to allow children to choose a partner of the same sex if they wish. Generally, there are few, if any, differences in the procedures or steps followed by the partners. If two girls choose to be partners, they can both curtsy, rather than have one girl bow.

If you use partners of the opposite sex, it is best not to allow any open objections by a student. You may allow anyone with a valid reason for not participating (injured foot, doctor's request not to engage in active play) to whisper that reason in your ear. Determine whether the reason is sufficient without any discussion. It is important that the student whispers the reason; other students who overhear an acceptable reason for not participating may decide to offer the same excuse.

Fortunately, many games and activities, even for upper elementary levels, do not require partners. "The Bunny Hop," "Alley Cat," "The Hora," "Who Has the Dime?" and "Shoo Fly" are among this group. They are excellent for party, camp, and school settings, where the requirement for pairing might stifle voluntary participation.

Recordings are available commercially for many of the more popular and traditional dances and games, such as "Hokey Pokey," "Pop Goes the Weasel," "Shoo Fly," "The Bunny Hop," "Alley Cat," and "The Mulberry Bush." Some of the recordings may be available in the golden oldies sections of record stores, in children's toy stores and departments that handle recordings for children, in recordings accompanying music books for the elementary school, and in school music and supply companies.

It is best to use recordings when performing these activities, but it is not always possible to do so. Music for most of the dances and activities has been included in the book for the convenience of those who can play the accompaniments, or wish to enlist others to play them. These accompaniments may be taped and used later with the children. Many times children can supply their own music simply by singing the song accompanying the dance or activity.

In a society where exercise and wholesome activity is important for the development of healthy citizens, the activities in this section should be welcomed and used liberally.

III–1   BLUEBIRD   Grades K–2

A simple circle game in which successive children are chosen to go in and out of the "windows" (raised, joined hands of children in the circle).

Objective: To follow a simple sequence of movements and to move rhythmically.

Formation: All children form a circle in the open space area except for one who is the "bluebird" and moves in and out of the circle underneath the raised, joined hands of the other children. On the verse, the "bluebird" selects a child from the circle. The two of them together go in and out under the joined hands.

Bluebird

Procedure:

1. Teach or review the above song.

2. Tell students that they are going to play a game with the song "Bluebird." Have the students walk to the open space area and form a circle, holding hands.

3. Appoint one child to be the "bluebird" and go to the center of the circle. Instruct all the children standing in the circle to join hands and raise them. As soon as the singing begins, the "bluebird" goes under the raised hands of the children in the circle. On the last phrase of the refrain, *Oh, Johnny, aren't you tired?* the "bluebird" selects another child from the circle to join him,

and together they go under the joined hands of the circle children during the verse. At the end of the verse, the first child chosen to be the "bluebird" joins the circle, leaving the second child to become the "bluebird" and repeat the above described activities.

III-2 SHOEMAKER'S DANCE Grades K-2

A simple dance with a series of movements by individuals or by partners.

Objective: To follow a simple sequence of rhythmic movements in cooperation with other children.

Formation: Children may stand in a circle or a line with or without partners, depending on your choice.

Shoemaker's Dance

Wind, wind, wind the thread, And wind, wind, wind the thread, And

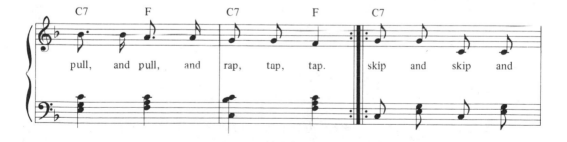

pull, and pull, and rap, tap, tap. skip and skip and

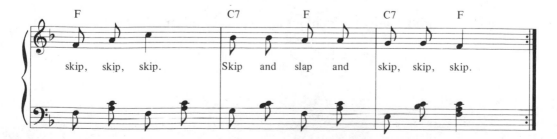

skip, skip, skip. Skip and slap and skip, skip, skip.

Procedure:

1. Teach the song.
2. Instruct children to form a circle. As they sing the song, have them do these motions:

   Wind, wind, wind the thread, Revolve closed fists around each other in a forward motion.

   Wind, wind, wind the thread, Revolve closed fists around each other in a backward motion.

   And pull and pull, Jerk elbows back vigorously as if pulling thread.

   And rap, tap, tap. Strike one clenched fist with the other three times.

   Skip and skip and skip, skip, skip. Skip and skip and skip, skip, skip. Skip around counterclockwise in the circle.

3. You could choose a child to go to the center of the circle to lead in the motions for the first half of the song. The child would rejoin the circle for the skipping.

Variation:

Children pair off, and stand in a double circle. They face each other to do the above motions and then join hands and skip around the circle on the second half of the song.

III–3   TEN LITTLE INDIANS   Grades K–2

This circle game requires children to stand or sit when their numbers are called.

Objective: To follow a simple sequence of rhythmic movements in cooperation with other children.

Formation: Children form a single circle and number off from one to ten.

Ten Little Indians

Procedure:

1. Teach or review the above song.
2. Have children form a circle and move counterclockwise during the first part of the song (*John Brown had a little Indian*). On the second part of the song (*One little, two little . . .*), children should number off from one to ten (there may be more than one of each number) and as each number is sung, the child or children with that assigned number should stoop down. On the repeat, when the numbers are sung in reverse order, the child or children who are assigned each number stand as it is sung.

III–4   THE MULBERRY BUSH   Grades K–2

A circle game in which children imitate the various chores usually done around the home or at work.

Objective: To participate in a series of rhythmical movements in cooperation with other children.

Formation: Children stand in a circle and do the motions suggested by the words of the song.

The Mulberry Bush

Here we go round the mul - berry bush, The mul - berry bush, the mul - berry bush. Here we go round the mul - berry bush, so ear - ly in the morn - ing.

Verse 1:

This is the way we wash our clothes,
  Wash our clothes, Wash our clothes.
This is the way we wash our clothes,
  So early Monday morning.

Verse 2:

This is the way we iron our clothes . . .
  So early Tuesday morning.

Verse 3:

This is the way we sweep the floor . . .
  So early Wednesday morning.

Verse 4:

This is the way we scrub the floor . . .
  So early Thursday morning.

Verse 5:

This is the way we mend our clothes . . .
  So early Friday morning.

Verse 6:

This is the way we dress ourselves . . .
  So early Saturday morning.

Verse 7:

This is the way we go to church . . .
  So early Sunday morning.

Procedure:

1. Teach or review the song above by singing one or more verses.
2. Ask the class to name some tasks that need to be done around the home. The tasks named may be those that they do or that other members of the family (or maid) do. List them on the blackboard and then select seven to include in this song, making sure that the words fit the music. See the suggested seven verses above for examples.
3. Organize the children in a circle in an open space area. On the first verse, *Here we go round the mulberry bush,* ask the children to join hands and walk or skip around in a circle. On the subsequent verses, ask them to engage in actions that are appropriate for the words of each verse.

Variation:

Have the children make a series of verses that are appropriate to another subject, and then make up motions to accompany the verses. Suitable topics may be: Caring for a pet, performing a certain type of work (farming, being a soldier), going to school.

III–5   LONDON BRIDGE IS
FALLING DOWN   Grades K–2

A singing game in which students march under an arch formed by the joined, raised hands of two students. At designated times, the arch comes down and entraps a student, who then joins a line behind one of the two students forming the arch. After all students have lined up behind the students forming the arch, the game ends with a tug-of-war between the two sides.

Objective: To participate in an organized group activity with a simple set of rules and movements.

Formation: Two students form an arch with their raised, joined hands while the rest of the students form a straight line to march through the arch. The straight line really marches in a circle so that after the last person files through the arch, the first person follows, going through the arch again.

London Bridge Is Falling Down

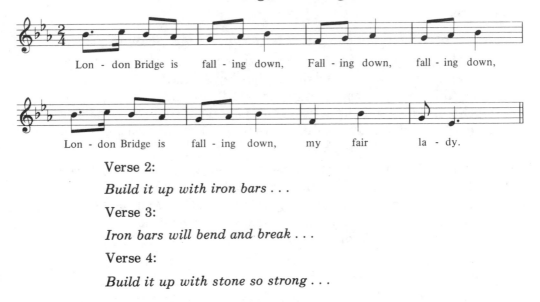

Lon - don Bridge is   fall - ing down,   Fall - ing down,   fall - ing down,

Lon - don Bridge is   fall - ing down,   my   fair   la - dy.

Verse 2:

Build it up with iron bars . . .

Verse 3:

Iron bars will bend and break . . .

Verse 4:

Build it up with stone so strong . . .

Procedure:

1. Teach or review the above song, singing all four verses.

2. Choose two children to join their raised hands to form an arch. The other children in the class form a line and march through the arch in a continuous line (with the first student following the last student who goes through) as they sing the verses. On the words *My fair lady*, the arch is dropped over the person entering the arch at that time. Each person who is caught must go behind one of the two people forming the arch (the first student caught goes behind the person forming one side of the arch, and the next person goes behind the other side, and so on. After all the children have been caught and have become a part of one of the two lines, the game ends with a tug-of-war.

III–6   THE FARMER IN THE DELL   Grades K–2

This is a circle singing game in which the last character chosen selects the next character to join the group in the center. On the last verse, all except the cheese rejoin the circle.

Objective: To participate in an organized singing game.

Formation: The children will form a circle in a large open classroom area.

The Farmer in the Dell

The farm - er in the dell, _____ the farm - er in the dell,

Hi - ho the der - ry - o, the farm - er in the dell. _____

Verse 2:	Verse 6:
The farmer takes a wife . . .	*Cat*
Verse 3:	Verse 7:
The wife takes the child . . .	*Rat*
Verse 4:	Verse 8:
Nurse	*Cheese*
Verse 5:	Verse 9:
Dog	*The cheese stands alone.*

Procedure:

1. Teach or review the above song.
2. The children form a large circle in the open space area of the classroom. One child is then chosen to stand in the center of the circle and be the farmer. The children in the circle join hands and move in a counterclockwise direction while they sing. On the second verse, the child in the center of the circle (who is the farmer) chooses one child from the circle to be the wife and join him in the center. On the third verse, the "wife" chooses another child

from the circle to be the child. The game continues in this fashion until the cheese is chosen. On the last verse, *The cheese stands alone*, all the children standing in the center of the circle, except the cheese, return to the circle.

3. The game may end here, or go through another complete cycle with the "cheese" becoming the "farmer" on the first verse.

Variation:

This variation is similar to the game above except that the children in the center, with the exception of the "cheese," do not rejoin the circle on the last verse. Instead, the song omits the last verse, *The cheese stands alone*, and goes back through the same sequence of characters. Instead of singing *The farmer takes a wife*, the words will change to *The farmer goes away*. On that verse, the farmer will rejoin the circle. The next verse will be *The wife goes away* and the "wife" rejoins the circle. Each character in succession "goes away" until no one is left but the cheese, and it is at this time that everyone sings *The cheese stands alone*. The game ends at this point.

III–7   SKIP TO MY LOU   Grades K–2

One child chooses a partner from the circle, and stands in front of her. On the chorus, they join hands and skip around the circle. On the verse, the first child rejoins the circle and the second continues the activity by standing in front of another child with whom she'll skip on the chorus.

Objective: To choose a partner and skip rhythmically around the circle.

Formation: Everyone stands in a circle in an open space area. One child is chosen to stand outside the circle initially to choose a partner and skip around the outer part of the circle.

Skip to My Lou

Procedure:

1. Teach the above song.

2. Ask the children to form a circle in a large open space area. One child is chosen to stand outside the circle and select a partner from the circle while the verse is being sung. The two children join hands on the refrain and skip around the circle. At the end of the refrain, the first child joins the circle and the second child walks around the circle while the verse is sung and selects a partner with whom he'll join hands and skip during the refrain. The game continues in this fashion until it is time to stop.

Variation:

Form a double circle, each with the same number of people, to facilitate the partner activity in the second half. On the verse, one circle walks in one direction with joined hands and the other circle walks in the opposite direction. On the refrain, the children in the outer circle pair off with the children in the second or inner circle (they should pair off with the person who happens to be directly in front of them). They join hands with their partners and skip around the circle. On the repeat of the refrain, the two circles form again and repeat the above movements.

III–8   WE'RE GOING TO THE CITY   Grades K–2

Four students in a straight line form a truck that goes around and through the circle. After four verses, a new "truck" is chosen to repeat the activities.

Objective: To move rhythmically in the interpretation of the words of the song.

Formation: A circle formation in the open space area of the classroom is necessary while four children form a truck and march around the outer part of the circle and under the clasped hands of children in the circle.

We're Going to the City

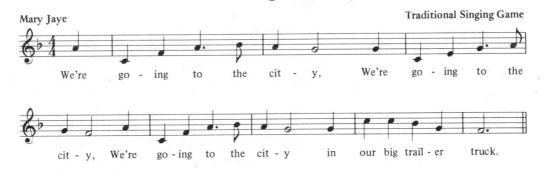

Mary Jaye   Traditional Singing Game

We're go - ing to the cit - y, We're go - ing to the

cit - y, We're go - ing to the cit - y in our big trail - er truck.

Verse 2:

Go in and out the tunnels. Go in and out the tunnels.
Go in and out the tunnels in our big trailer truck.

Verse 3:

We'll drive across the bridges,

Verse 4:

It's time to change the driver,

"We're Going to the City" from *Making Music Your Own,*
© 1966, 1971 Silver Burdett Company. Reprinted by permission.

Procedure:

1. Teach or review all four verses of the above song.

2. If there is enough room, ask all students except three or four to come up and form a circle, holding hands. The remaining three or four students will form the "truck." They stand in a straight

line, one behind the other, with the back two or three students placing their hands on the shoulders of the person in front of them. The front person is the leader of the truck.

3. The game is as follows:

Verse 1: The "truck" walks around the outside of the circle.

Verse 2: The people in the circle lift their clasped hands for the "truck" to go in and out underneath their hands.

Verse 3: The circle members keep their hands held high so that the "truck" can go under one pair of hands and exit the circle under the clasped hands on the opposite side. There is time to do this twice.

Verse 4: Each member of the "truck" finds someone in the circle and exchanges places with him. The old "truck" members become part of the circle, and the selected old circle members become the new "truck."

This sequence is repeated as many times as you wish.

III–9   HOW DO YOU DO
MY PARTNER?   Grades 1–3

This is a circle game using partners and a series of simple movements, such as bowing to partners, joining right arms and swinging, and skipping around in a circle.

Objective: To move rhythmically while going through a simple series of steps.

Formation: Children select partners and stand in a double circle in an open space area. The boys make up the outer circle, and the girls make up the inner circle.

How Do You Do My Partner?

How do you do my part - ner? How do you do to - day? ____

Will you dance in a cir - cle if I show you the way?

Refrain:

Tra - la - la - la - la, _____ Tra - la - la - la - la, _____

Tra - la - la - la - la, _____ Tra - la - la - la - la - la.

Procedure:

1. Teach the above song.

2. Organize children in a double circle. They should be paired off (preferably boy–girl partners); half of each pair should be in the outer circle (the boy) and the other half should be in the inner circle by her partner. If there are more boys than girls, or vice versa, children of the same sex can pair off.

3. Partners (one from each circle, inner and outer) face each other and do these steps on the first half of the song:

   How do you do my partner, Boys bow and girls curtsy.

   How do you do today? Boys bow and girls curtsy again.

   Will you dance in a circle if I show you the way? Join right elbows with partner and swing around in a circle.

   On the refrain (*tra-la-las*), partners join hands in a promenade position and skip around in a circle.

4. The activity can end here, or if preferred, it can continue by asking the inner circle to move down one person to the right so that everyone now has a new partner, ready to repeat the entire sequence above.

III–10   MUFFIN MAN   Grades 1–3

This singing game begins with one child choosing a partner by standing in front of another child. On the second verse they join both hands and skip around in a small circle. The two-verse sequence is repeated as each child now chooses a new partner. This continues until all children have been chosen.

Objective: To choose a new partner on each two-verse sequence and to move rhythmically in a circle with the partner.

Formation: One person comes to the open space area and selects another to be his partner. They join hands and swing around in a circle. Each of these partners will find a new partner to swing. This continues until the entire class is in the open space area with joined hands, swinging around.

Muffin Man

Oh, do you know the muf-fin man, the muf-fin man, the muf-fin man? Oh, do you know the muf-fin man who lives in Dru-ry Lane?

Verse 2:

Oh yes, I know the muffin man, the muffin man, the muffin man.
Oh yes, I know the muffin man that lives in Drury Lane.

Procedure:

1. Teach both verses of the song above.

2. To teach the singing game, tell students that you are going to do something special as they continue singing the song, and that before they are through, the entire class will be in the open space area with a partner, dancing in a circle. As children sing the first verse, select a student by standing in front of him. On the second verse, join both hands and skip, or move around in a circle with a side step. At the end of these two verses the class will continue to sing while you and your partner select new partners from the class by standing in front of them. On the second verse, both of you will join hands with your new partners and move in a circle with a side step or skip. All four dancers will then seek new partners with whom to dance. The game continues in this fashion until the entire class is in the open space area. Careful attention needs to be given to the two-verse sequence in which the last members of the class are called up. If there is an odd number of people in the class, you will have to participate so that everyone will have a partner. If there is an even number, then you will not have to participate.

   If there are twenty-six people dancing and only six people left in their seats to be chosen on the next and last two-verse sequence, have the children choose the remaining six seated students and the remaining twenty dancers pair off with each other in the open space area so that everyone is dancing.

III–11   BOW, BOW, BELINDA   Grades 1–3

This singing game uses the reel formation and several of the simpler movements used in square dancing.

Objective: To participate in an organized singing game using a simple sequence of steps and rhythmic movements.

Formation: This singing game requires a reel formation in an open classroom space.

Bow, Bow, Belinda

Bow, Bow, Bow, Be-lin - da. Bow, Bow, Bow, Be-lin - da.

Bow, Bow, Bow, Be-lin - da. Won't you be my dar - ling?

Verse 2:

Right hand up, Belinda. Right hand up, Belinda
Right hand up, Belinda. Won't you be my darling?

Verse 3:

Left hand up, Belinda . . .

Verse 4:

Both hands up, Belinda . . .

Verse 5:

Do-si-do, O Belinda . . .

Verse 6:

Promenade, O Belinda . . .

Procedure:

1. Teach or review all the verses of the above song.
2. Select eight to twelve students to come to the front and learn the dance. Remind the other students that they will need to pay attention as they may be asked to do the dance next. Students selected to come to the front will stand in two straight lines with partners in opposite lines facing each other. Have partners hold

hands (to make sure they have located each other) and then step
back about five or six steps each so that there are about eight to
ten feet between the two lines.

3. Have the students walk through the following steps without the
   music:

   Verse 1: Partners walk forward, bow, and walk back to their
   places. There is time to do this twice.

   Verse 2: Partners join right hands and turn clockwise.

   Verse 3: Partners join left hands and turn counterclockwise.

   Verse 4: Partners join both hands and turn clockwise.

   Verse 5: Partners fold their arms in front of their bodies and
   walk toward their partners, passing right shoulder to
   right shoulder, back to back, left shoulder to left shoulder, and back to their places (do-si-do). It is important
   that each partner continues to face in the same direction while doing this movement.

   Verse 6: Partners hold hands in a skating position (crossed in
   front) and walk around the room (head couple, designated before the singing game begins, leads).

4. After walking through the motions, let the class sing the song
   while the dancers do the motions.

5. Select another group from the seated students to dance while
   the first group rests and sings.

Variation:

Ask the class to create new verses with new steps.

III–12   RIG-A-JIG-JIG   Grades 1–3

This is a circle game in which successive children choose a partner with whom they will skip on the second half of the song.

Objective: To participate in an organized singing game using basic movements.

Formation: Children form a circle in an open classroom area. One or two children at a time move around the circle using various basic movements.

Rig-A-Jig-Jig

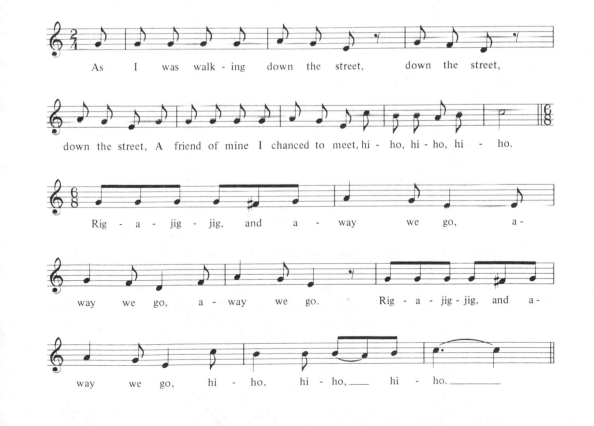

Procedure:

1. Teach or review the above song.
2. Have children sitting or standing in a circle. Choose one child to walk around the circle during the first half of the song (up to the 6/8 time). This child chooses a partner to skip or gallop with him on the second half of the song that begins with *Rig-a-jig-jig.*
3. The child chosen as the skipping (or galloping) partner announces what movement he will do while singing the first half of the song, as the first child joins the circle. If the child who remains up to do a motion chooses marching, then the class will sing *As I was marching down the street . . .* The student will choose a partner to skip (or gallop) with him on the second part of the song beginning with *Rig-a-jig-jig.* The game continues with the second selected child choosing a movement for the class to sing while she performs it. Again, the youngster chooses a partner to skip with on the second half of the song. The same motion of skipping or galloping will always be done on this part of the song while the movement on the first half varies according to each child's wish. This process continues until you decide it is time to stop.

III–13   MAKE A PRETTY MOTION   Grades 1–3

A simple imitative singing game in which one child demonstrates a motion on the first verse and the others join in on the second verse.

Objective: To create movements and move rhythmically.

Formation: No special formation is required. One child may be called to the front of the class to demonstrate and lead in a movement of his choosing, while the others stand beside their desks and imitate him. If desired, a circle formation may be used with the leader in the center.

Make a Pretty Motion

1. Make a pret-ty mo - tion, fol-ly - fay, make a pret-ty mo - tion,

fol-ly - fay, Make a pret-ty mo - tion, fol-ly - fay, so rise, sug - ar, rise,

Verse 2:

Mighty pretty motion, follyfay,
Mighty pretty motion, follyfay,
Mighty pretty motion, follyfay,
So rise, Sugar, rise.

Procedure:

1. Teach both verses of the above song.

2. Organize the children in circular formation in an open space area.

3. If the class is relatively inexperienced, you may want to be the first person to demonstrate a movement, and then have the class join with the motion on the second verse. Otherwise, a student may be chosen to be the first leader. Whoever is the leader should stand in the center of the circle and demonstrate a motion on the first stanza while the class sings. As indicated above, the class imitates the movement as they sing the second stanza.

4. Choose another leader to take the place of the first leader. Sing the two verses again, with the chosen student demonstrating a motion for the class to imitate on the second verse.

5. The game continues in this fashion until all students have had a chance to be the leader or until you determine it is over.

Variation:

The words can be changed to reflect a particular subject or category, such as:

   a. Animals: I'm a little dog, bow-bow-bow
                    I'm a little lamb, Baa, baa, baa.

   b. Transportation: I'm a little bus, beep, beep, beep.
                           I'm an airplane, zoom, zoom, zoom.

   c. Rhythm Instruments: I'm a tambourine, clink, clink, clink.
                              I'm a little drum, boom, boom, boom.

III–14   JINGLE AT THE WINDOWS   Grades 1–3

Children form a circle and perform simple movements, such as walking around in a circle and swinging partners with hooked elbows.

Objective: To participate in an organized activity consisting of simple movements.

Formation: All the children form a circle in the open space area of the classroom.

Jingle at the Windows

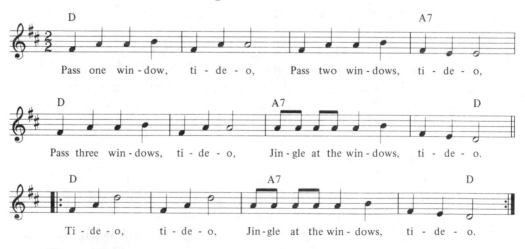

Procedure:

1. Teach or review the above song. Notice the two dots at the beginning and end of the last line. These mean that the last line is to be sung twice before ending the song.

2. All children participating in this circle game must pair off (preferably boy and girl) and form a large single circle. (You may wish to have everyone form a single circle first with boys and girls alternating, and then have them identify their partners.)

3. Ask all the children in the circle to face right. Each child should place his left hand on the right shoulder of the child in front of him. On measures 1 through 8 (the first two lines or phrases of the song), children sing and march in the direction they are facing. Emphasize good rhythmic marching steps by each child.

4. In measures 9 through 12, partners hook right elbows and swing around. In the repeat of measures 9 through 12, partners hook left elbows and swing around.

5. The entire song may be repeated as many times as you like. If it is repeated, children can change partners simply by having all the girls step one boy over.

III–15   SANTY MALONEY   Grades 1–3

This is a circle game in which children do the motions indicated by the words in each verse and join hands and skip around during the chorus.

Objective: To participate in an organized singing game by doing a series of rhythmic movements.

Formation: Children form a circle in an open space area in the classroom.

Santy Maloney

Verse 2:

Put your hand on your shoulders, Put your hand on your shoulders,
Put your hand on your shoulders as we go round about.

Verse 3:

Put your hand in your pockets . . .

Verse 4:

Nod your head to the music . . .

Verse 5:

Tap your foot to the music . . .

The chorus after each verse above is:

Here we go, Santy Maloney, Here we go, Santy Maloney,
Here we go, Santy Maloney as we go round about.

The tune to the chorus is the same as for the verse.

Procedure:

1. Teach or review the above song, singing the chorus after each verse.

2. Organize children in a circle formation in an open space area in the classroom. All children skip on the first verse and chorus, going in a counterclockwise direction.

3. On each subsequent verse, the children stop skipping and do the motion suggested by the words. For example, they stand still in the circle, facing toward the center, and put their hands on their shoulders on verse 2; they put their hands in their pockets on verse 3 (or pretend to if they have no pockets), and so on. Between each verse, they face right and skip around the circle on each chorus.

Variation:

Children may wish to make up new verses that describe movements they are to do simultaneously with singing.

III–16   CLAP YOUR HANDS   Grades 1–3

In this singing game, children do the motions suggested by the words and run on tiptoe during the chorus.

Objective: To move rhythmically in cooperation with other children to the words of the song.

Formation: Children form a circle in the open space area of the classroom.

Clap Your Hands

Procedure:

1. Teach or review the above song.

2. Tell children that the song is divided into two parts, a verse and a chorus. The words to the verse change each time the song is sung, but the chorus is the same each time. Ask children to listen to the song as they sing it again to determine where the tune changes. They should guess the ninth measure where the *las* are sung. Identify the first half of the song as the verse and the second half as the chorus.

3. Invite them to make up at least three more verses besides the ones given here. Each of these three verses should suggest a movement they can make while standing in a circle. Typical verses might be:

   Touch your toes, bend right down
   Touch them all right now (sing both lines twice).

Bow, bow, bow so low, Bow so low right now.
Bow, bow, bow so low, Bow so low right now.

Nod, nod, nod your heads, Nod your heads together.
Nod, nod, nod your heads, Nod your heads together.

Up, down, move your arms, Up and down together.
Up, down, move your arms, Up and down together.

4. Have children form a circle in the open space area of the classroom. Review the sequence of movements for each verse they have decided upon. After each verse, they are to tiptoe (or skip, or some other locomotor movement) on the chorus in a counterclockwise direction.

III–17   HOKEY POKEY   Grades 1–3

This well-known singing game is done in a circle formation and movements follow the words of the song.

Objective: To participate in a singing game using rhythmic movements.

Formation: Children stand in a circle formation in an open space area of the classroom.

Hokey Pokey

1. You put your right hand in,— You put your right hand out,— You put your right hand in,— And you shake it all a-bout, And then you do the Ho-key Po-key, And you turn your-self a-round, And that's what it's all a-bout. *Hey!*
(Spoken)

Verse 2:

You put your left hand in . . .

Verse 3:

Right foot

Verse 4:	Verse 6:
Left foot	*Left hip*
Verse 5:	Verse 7:
Right hip	*Whole self*

Procedure:

1. Teach or review the first two verses of the above song.

2. Ask all students to hold up their right hands and then their left ones. This procedure may be done with their feet and other body parts (touch the right ear, eye, left ear, eye, and so on.)

3. Ask what kind of motion might be done to the phrase *You do the hokey pokey*, and have students demonstrate. Generally, the motion done for this phrase is to hold up the index fingers at about shoulder height and sway the hips from side to side; however, you may use any motion that you and the students decide on.

4. Sing the first two verses again with the motions indicated by the words of the song: right hand in front, moving it in rhythm to the beat; right hand in back; right hand in front; do the hokey pokey motion decided upon; turn around; clap on the beat beginning with the first word of *That's what it's all about*, and end on *Hey!*

5. Write the order of the body parts that will be used in the singing game on the blackboard.

6. Have students form a circle in the open space area of the classroom and perform all verses of the singing game.

III–18   THE NOBLE DUKE OF YORK   Grades 2–4

This singing game requires a reel formation. Each of the partners in succession will hold hands and move sideways the length of the reel and back. At this point, they will cast off and form an arch, under which all the other partners pass.

Objective: To participate in a singing game using rhythmic movements.

Formation: A reel formation, consisting of approximately twelve people per reel, is formed in the open space area of the classroom.

The Noble Duke of York

Oh, the no-ble Duke of York,   He   had ten thou-sand men,   He

marched them up to the top of the hil, And he marched them down a - gain.

Verse 2:

Oh, when you're up, you're up.
And when you're down, you're down.
But when you're only halfway up,
You're neither up nor down.

Procedure:

1. Teach both verses of the above song.

2. Select twelve students to come to the front and stand in a reel formation (two straight lines of six each, with partners in opposite lines facing each other).

3. Have the twelve students walk through these motions before doing them with the music:

Verse 1: The head couple (designated by you and positioned at
one end of the reel) joins hands and does a side step up
and back down the reel.

Verse 2: Partners separate and cast off (a square dance term
that means that each partner goes behind her line and
the lines follow their leaders to the foot of the reel.
Once the head couple arrives at the foot, they join
hands, making an arch, beneath which each of the
other partners in the reel will meet, join hands, and
pass through.

At this point, the old head couple should be at the foot of the reel
and a new head couple at the top ready to go through the above
sequence of movements again. The game continues until all couples have gone through the movements for verses one and two.

III–19   POP GOES THE WEASEL   Grades 2–5

Small circles of four are arranged in a larger circle with one couple in each smaller circle moving to the next one on the word *pop!*

Objective: To perform a simple American folk dance in a rhythmic
manner.

Formation: All participating children should be in an open space
area organized in small circles of four (two sets of partners), which, in turn, form a larger circle. From twelve to
forty students may participate simultaneously, depending on the size of the open space area.

Pop Goes the Weasel

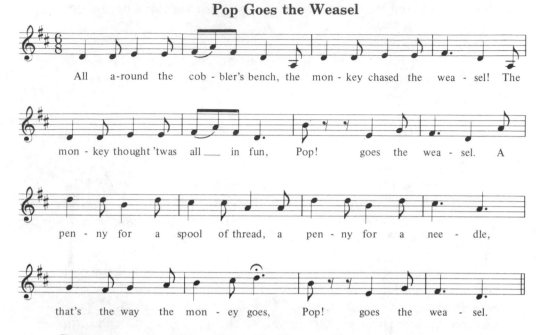

All a-round the cob-bler's bench, the mon-key chased the wea-sel! The mon-key thought 'twas all __ in fun, Pop! goes the wea-sel. A pen-ny for a spool of thread, a pen-ny for a nee-dle, that's the way the mon-ey goes, Pop! goes the wea-sel.

Dance steps for "Pop Goes the Weasel!"

Students arrange themselves in small circles (or squares) of four. These small circles of four are organized in a larger circle. In effect, a double circle will be formed with partners in different circles. Two sets of partners join hands to form the smaller circles of four described above.

Measures 1–4: Each circle of four joins hands and moves to the left for eight steps.

Measures 5–8: Each circle of four then reverses directions and moves to the right for eight steps.

Measures 9–10: Members of each small circle take four steps to the center of their circle and raise their joined hands.

Measures 11–12: They take four steps back lowering their hands.

Measures 13–16: The couple facing clockwise in each small circle raises their joined hands so that the other couple, facing counter-clockwise, can go under their raised hands on the word *pop!* and move on to join another small circle to repeat all of the above steps as the song is sung again. This procedure should be repeated until all couples return to their original circles.

Procedure:

1. Teach or review the above song so that the children can sing it fluently.

2. If children have never done the dance before, ask a group of about twelve to sixteen students to come to the open space area. Arrange half of them in an outer circle and half of them in an inner circle facing each other to identify their partners. As soon as they have identified their partners (the two people in opposite circles facing each other), have two sets of adjacent partners (four people) join hands to form the small circles of four.

3. Walk through the above steps in the dance, helping those who need it. It is better not to use the music at this stage so you can stop the group to explain or demonstrate as necessary.

4. After the group is able to go through the series of steps, ask the group to sing the song and clap their hands while they do the dance.

5. If the entire group is not participating in the dance, exchange groups so that the present dancers take their seats and sing and the seated group performs the dance. If there is space, you may prefer to have the original group continue dancing with the new members forming groups of four to join in the larger circle.

III–20   SHOO, FLY   Grades 2–5

This is a circle folk dance that involves a simple sequence of movements and features an inversion of the circle and a subsequent return to the normal circle position.

Objective: To perform an organized activity involving simple rules and a simple series of steps in a rhythmic manner.

Formation: Groups of five (or another odd number of three or seven) form circles in an open space area. If all students in the group are to participate, you may have to join in as there must be an odd number in each circle.

Shoo, Fly

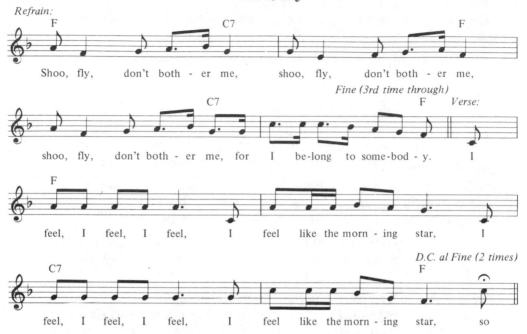

Refrain:

Shoo, fly, don't both-er me, shoo, fly, don't both-er me,

shoo, fly, don't both-er me, for I be-long to some-bod-y. I

Fine (3rd time through)

Verse:

feel, I feel, I feel, I feel like the morn - ing star, I

D.C. al Fine (2 times)

feel, I feel, I feel, I feel like the morn - ing star, so

Dance steps for "Shoo, Fly"

Students organize themselves into circles of five and join hands. (If there are students left over after organizing circles of five, it is permissible for one circle to contain three or seven students.)

Measure 1: Students in each circle walk toward the center of the circle raising their joined hands high as they go.

Measure 2: Students walk back to their original places, lowering their joined hands as they walk.

Measure 3: Same as measure 1.

Measure 4: Same as measure 2.

Measures 5–8: One student in each circle (designated before the beginning of the dance) walks forward (hands are still joined) and goes under the joined hands of the two people opposite her (the second and third people from her) leading the rest of the circle through. The two people under whose hands all are going do not drop hands, but must pivot around to complete the inversion of the circle. As soon as the circle is inverted with all members facing outward, the circle should be enlarged as much as possible.

Measures 1–4 (repeat): Repeat the steps outlined in measures 1–4 in which the members of the circle, which is now inverted, walk backward to the center and back out twice.

Measures 5–8 (second time): The designated student who led in the inversion of the circle now leads the group under the joined hands of the two people opposite her (the second and third people from her).

As the circle is inverted, they will have to walk backwards under the joined hands. Remember, as before, that all continue to hold hands as they restore the circle to its original position. As soon as all people have gone under the joined hands of the two circle members and they have pivoted around without dropping hands, the circle should be stretched to its widest diameter.

Measures 1–4 (second repeat): Repeat the steps originally outlined for measures 1–4.

Procedure:

1. Teach or review "Shoo Fly." Indicate that this repeat is somewhat different from most in that the entire song is sung twice, ending on *Fine* after the refrain is sung the third time.

2. Select five students to come to the open space area to assist you in demonstrating the steps of the dance outlined above. Walk them through the steps, stopping to give help where needed. The most difficult part seems to be in measures 5–8, where the circle is inverted and then restored to its original position in the repeat.

3. After walking through the steps with the demonstration group, ask the group to sing (or, if possible, a recording or the piano may be played) while they do the entire dance.

4. Form circles of five with the entire group (one circle may have to contain three or seven students to use everyone). Before they all do the dance with the music, have them walk through the sequence of steps, paying particular attention to the steps in measures 5–8. As soon as they are able, let all do the dance with the music.

III–21   PAW-PAW PATCH   Grades 2–5

Boys and girls stand in parallel lines facing each other. A different lead girl is featured each time the series of four verses is repeated, with the entire group participating at designated times.

Objective: To participate in an organized game in cooperation with a group in a rhythmic manner.

Formation: Reel formation is required. Have eight to sixteen students, boys in one line and girls in another, facing each other. An open space area is required.

Paw-Paw Patch

1. Where, oh where is sweet lit-tle Nel - lie? Where, oh where is sweet lit-tle Nel - lie? Where, oh where is sweet lit-tle Nel - lie? Way down yon-der in the paw - paw patch.

Verse 2:

Come on, boys, and let's go find her,
Come on, boys, and let's go find her,
Come on, boys, and let's go find her,
Way down yonder in the paw-paw patch.

Verse 3:

Pickin' up paw-paws,

> *putt'n 'em in her basket . . .*

Verse 4:

Here she comes, we'll go with her . . .

Procedure:

1. Teach or review the above song, singing all four verses.

2. Select ten students to come to the open space area to help you demonstrate the game. Five of the students, who should be boys, line up in a straight line facing the other five students, who should be girls. This is called a reel formation. There should be approximately eight feet between the two lines. Walk through these movements without the music:

Game movements:

Verse 1: The girl at the head of the line (her left shoulder should be toward the end of the line) turns and skips behind the line of girls and back to her place through the center of the two lines.

Verse 2: The same girl, who is "Little Nellie," skips the same route as in verse one, but this time the line of boys follows her behind the line of girls, resuming their original position as they pass the foot of the girls' line and skip toward the head of the reel. Each time the group sings *Come on, boys*, they move their hands as though to wave the rest of the group on.

Verse 3: "Little Nellie" (the same girl from verses 1 and 2) walks down and back up the center of the two lines pretending to pick up paw-paws as the others clap in rhythm.

Verse 4: "Nellie" and her partner (the head couple) turn away from each other, skipping behind their respective lines with the girls following "Nellie," and the boys following her partner. The head couple meets at the foot of the reel, and forms an arch, while the others pass through and return to place. "Nellie" and her partner remain at the foot of the reel, and the game is repeated with a new "Nellie" and her partner. This repetition continues until all the girls have had a chance to be "Nellie."

Do not walk through all the repetitions. Generally, once or twice will be sufficient for most of the group to grasp the sequence of steps.

3. Have the demonstration group do the game as the group sings the song.

4. Call up as many of the entire group as the open space area will allow, forming reels of anywhere from four to six couples. The same number should be in each reel, if possible, so that when the game ends, all girls will have played "Nellie."

5. If you wish, instead of featuring "Little Nellie" each time, the group may prefer to change it to "Little Willie" so that the boys are the featured participants instead of the girls.

III–22   OLD JOE CLARK   Grades 2–6

A circle dance using partners and involving a simple sequence of movements is used for this song.

Objective: To move rhythmically through a series of dance steps in cooperation with a group.

Formation: All participants form a large circle in an open space area facing counterclockwise. The circle is composed of boy and girl partners so that every other person in the circle is a girl.

Old Joe Clark

Verse 2:

Old Joe Clark <u>had</u> a mule, His <u>name</u> was Morgan <u>Brown</u>,
And <u>every</u> tooth in <u>that</u> mule's head, was <u>sixteen</u> inches <u>round</u>.
CHORUS

Verse 3:

Old Joe Clark had a yellow cat, She would neither sing or pray,
She stuck her head in the buttermilk jar, And washed her sins away.
CHORUS

Verse 4:

Old Joe Clark had a house Fifteen stories high,
And every story in that house, Was filled with chicken pie.
CHORUS

Verse 5:

I went down to old Joe's house, He invited me to supper,
I stubbed my toe on the table leg, And stuck my nose in the butter.
CHORUS

Verse 6:

Sixteen horses in my team, The leaders they are blind,
And every time the sun goes down, There's a pretty girl on my mind.
CHORUS

Verse 7:

I wish I had a sweetheart, I'd put her on a shelf,
And every time she'd smile at me, I'd get up there myself.
CHORUS

Dance Steps:

1. Partners stand in a single circle facing counterclockwise with the boys in front of the girls, who place their left hands on the right shoulders of their partners.

2. All march around in the circle during the verse, or they may choose a particular step to do as they move in a counterclockwise direction around the circle.

3. Partners join right elbows and swing their partners around during the first four measures of the chorus, ending with the girls standing in front of their partners. The boys then turn to the girls standing behind them, and they join elbows. They swing around with the new partner for the last four measures, ending with the girls standing behind them.

4. The dance continues in this fashion with the new girl partner putting her left hand on the right shoulder of the boy. The activity continues until the original partners meet.

Procedure:

1. Teach or review the above song. Do as many verses as desired. Note that certain words have been underlined in verses two through seven. These underlined words (or syllables) indicate the first beat of each measure as the words vary in rhythmic pattern from verse to verse.

2. Arrange the group with partners (boy–girl) standing in a single circle facing counterclockwise. Walk through the steps described above without music.

3. Do the dance with music after the group is able to walk through it successfully without music. Music may be furnished by having the group sing as they dance (if they do not know all the verses, they can sing the one or two they do know over and over), or by playing a commercial recording of the music, or a recording made by a local pianist or chorus.

III–23   AROUND THE CHRISTMAS TREE   Grades 2–6

This simple circle game requires partners and uses a series of simple steps.

Objective: To participate in a circle game in a rhythmic manner.

Formation: Partners form a double circle, one partner in each circle, in a large open space area.

Around the Christmas Tree

Swedish Folk Song

1. Christ - mas a - gain, It's Christ - mas a - gain! We're hap - py so we dance and ca - per, Glad when we see the bright Christ - mas tree, With gifts wrapped in col - ored pa - per.

Verse 2:

Do come and see the gay Christmas tree,
With strings of twinkling lights we wound it.
Now for some fun, Come on, ev'ry one,
We'll join hands and dance around it.

Dance Movements:

Children form a double circle with boys in the outer circle and girls in the inner circle facing each other initially.

Verse 1: For the first four measures, each person slaps his upper legs on beat one and then his partner's hands on beats two and three. Partners join hands in a promenade position and skip in a counterclockwise direction around the circle for the last four measures.

Verse 2: Do the same movements as described for verse 1.

Procedure:

1. Teach the above song, singing both verses.

2. Arrange the children in a double circle with partners in different circles facing each other as described above. Walk through the steps described above without the music.

3. After children are able to walk through the steps successfully, have them do the dance with the music (as they sing, as someone plays the piano, or as a recording is played).

III–24   THE JOLLY MILLER   Grades 2–6

This game uses a double circle and partners, who change at the end of each sequence.

Objective: To participate in an organized game in a rhythmic manner.

Formation: Children form a double circle with partners in an open space area.

The Jolly Miller

There was a jol-ly mill-er and he lived by him-self, As the wheel went round he made his wealth, One hand in the hop-per and the oth-er in the sack, The boy steps for-ward and the girl steps back.

Game Movements:

Partners line up in a double circle (boys in the outer circle and girls in the inner circle) holding hands in promenade fashion and facing in a counterclockwise direction.

Measures 1–4: March forward in a counterclockwise direction, one step per beat.

Measures 5–6: Partners release hands so that on beat one of measure five (on the word *hand*) boys slap their right hands with the girls' left hands. Both of the partners immediately pivot around toward the outside in a full circle to slap their opposite hands together (boys' left hands with girls' right hands).

Measures 7–8: Each boy steps forward to claim the girl who was part of the couple ahead of him, as the girl steps back to become partners with the boy who was part of the couple behind. Repeat the song and dance as often as you wish.

Procedure:

1. Teach the song above.

2. Arrange the group in partners forming a double circle as described above. All should be facing counterclockwise, holding hands in a promenade position with their partners. Walk through the series of steps outlined above until they are able to do them without hesitation.

3. Do the game as the children sing the song, or hear a recording of the music. The game is repeated as often as you wish or until children return to their original partners.

III–25   RIGHT HEEL, LEFT   Grades 2–6

Two lines of partners face each other and join hands. They alternately point right and left heels while hopping on the other foot. On subsequent verses, the lead couple does designated movements, such as skipping, hopping, and the like.

Objective: To participate in a large group organized activity using rhythmic movement.

Formation: Students stand in two straight lines with partners facing each other from opposite lines, in an open space area. From eight to sixteen students form each dance set, though there can be as many sets as the open space permits.

Right Heel, Left

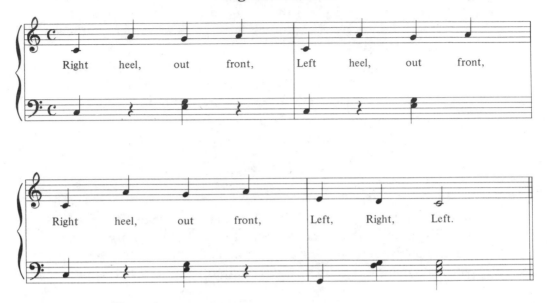

Right   heel,   out   front,   Left   heel,   out   front,

Right   heel,   out   front,   Left,   Right,   Left.

Verse 2:

The first lady skips right down the line,
Takes her place at the foot of the line.

Verse 3:

The first gentleman skips right down the line,
Takes his place at the foot of the line.

Dance Steps:

From eight to sixteen students stand in two straight lines of equal numbers with partners facing each other in opposite lines.

Verse 1: Students hop on the left foot as they point right heels outward on the first beat of measure one. On the first beat of measure two, they point the left heel out as they bring the right heel back with a hop. On the first beat of the third measure, they put the right heel forward as they bring back the left heel with a hop. On beats one, two, and three of measure four, they do a quick left heel forward, right heel forward, left heel forward with quick hopping motions.

Verse 2: The girl at the head of the line skips down to the foot and takes her place at the end of the girls' line.

Verse 3: The boy at the head of the line skips down to the foot and takes his place at the end of the boys' line.

Continue the dance, repeating the verses until all the children in the set have had a turn skipping down the line.

Procedure:

1. Teach the above song, singing all three verses.

2. Arrange eight to sixteen children in two straight lines with partners facing each other. Walk through the steps of the dance described above until the group is able to perform them successfully.

3. Perform the dance with the children singing the song. Repeat the sequence until all children in the set have skipped in verses two and three. Several different sets of dancers may participate simultaneously.

III–26   BLEKING   Grades 2–6

This is a Swedish folk dance in which partners hold hands facing each other and do a series of hops on one foot while putting the other heel forward. The second half of the dance uses a step-hop movement.

Objective: To participate in a large group folk dance in a rhythmic fashion.

Formation: Children pair off and face each other in an open space area. The partners may be organized in a larger circle, in a straight line or in any other fashion that is suitable for the space available.

Bleking

Swedish Folk Dance

Dance Movements:

Partners stand facing each other, holding both hands. Partners may be organized around a circle if desired.

Measures 1-8:

The partners jump as they put their right heels forward on beat one. They then reverse the step, putting their left heels forward as they jump on beat two. In measure two, they do three of these steps (right heel forward, left heel forward, right heel forward) in quick succession on the first beat and a half. These same steps are repeated three more times.

Measures 9–16:

Partners join right hands and hold them in an upraised position as they move in a clockwise direction using a step-hop pattern throughout the remainder of the song.

Procedure:

1. Rehearse the two basic steps that are used throughout the dance. One step involves jumping on one foot while putting the other heel forward and then reversing the feet. The students should do this several times in succession without partners until they feel comfortable with it. The other step is a simple step-hop pattern in which they step on the left foot and hop while the right foot is in the air; then they step on the right foot and hop while the left foot is in the air. They continue in this fashion alternating left and right feet.

2. Arrange the group into partners in an open space area. The partners may be organized around a circle or placed haphazardly around the area. Go through the steps without the music at first.

3. After the group walks through the steps, have them do the steps with the music, which may be played on a piano or organ, or a recorded tape.

III–27   CHILDREN'S POLKA   Grades 2–6

This is a partner game that involves a series of slide steps, stamps, and clapping.

Objective: To participate in an organized game in a rhythmic manner.

Formation: Partners may be arranged around a large double circle in an open space area or stand anywhere as long as they have room to do the steps without colliding with other partners.

Children's Polka

German Folk Game

Oh, slide and slide, and stamp, stamp, stamp, And slide and slide, and

stamp, stamp, stamp. Your knees, your hands, and one, two, three! Your

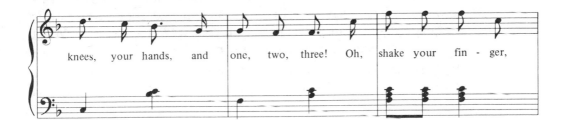

knees, your hands, and one, two, three! Oh, shake your fin - ger,

shake your fin - ger, turn a - round_ and _ stamp, stamp, stamp!

From *Music Activities for Retarded Children* by David R. Ginglend and Winifred E. Stiles. Copyright © 1965 by Abingdon Press. Used by permission.

Dance Steps:

Measures 1–4 (first time and repeat): *Oh, slide and slide, and stamp, stamp, stamp,*

Do two step-togethers (step to right with right foot and slide left foot so that it is beside the right foot; the opposite foot is used by the partner) in the direction agreed upon by the class; stamp three times as indicated by the words. On the repeat, do the same series of steps, but in the opposite direction.

Measures 5–8: *Your knees, your hands, and one, two, three!*

Slap knees, clap hands, then pat the partner's hands three times.

Measures 9–10: *Shake your finger,*

Put the left hand on the hip and shake the finger of the right hand at the partner.

Measures 11–12: *Turn around and stamp, stamp, stamp!*

Turn around and stamp three times with alternate feet.

Procedure:

1. Demonstrate the step-slide together that begins the above dance, and ask the group to practice the step standing in front of their seats.

2. Pair the children off and arrange them in an open space area in a double circle or in any other way as long as they have ample room to move through the dance steps without a collision. Walk through the sequence of steps without the music.

3. As soon as they are familiar with the sequence of steps, do the dance with the music (recorded on a tape or played by someone on the piano).

III–28   DANCE OF GREETING   Grades 2–6

A Danish folk dance performed in a circle formation features the repetition of a short series of steps between each verse.

Objective: To participate in an organized dance in a rhythmic fashion.

Formation: Children pair off and form a single circle in an open space area.

Dance of Greeting

(Refrain)

Verse 2:

Join hands and circle left, Circle left together.
Join hands and circle left, Circle left together.

(Refrain)

Verse 3:

Join arms and swing around, Swing around together.
Join arms and swing around, Swing around together.

(Refrain)

Dance Steps:

Refrain: Steps follow the words.

Measure 1: Turn to face the partner and bow.

Measure 2: Turn around to face the person on the opposite side and bow.

Measure 3: Stamp twice (at the same time that the words are sung).

Measure 4: Turn completely around.

Verse 1: All those in the circle join hands and skip or shuffle to the right.

Verse 2: All those in the circle join hands and skip or shuffle to the left.

Verse 3: Partners hook right elbows and swing around together.

Procedure:

1. Teach or review the above song. The song begins and ends with the refrain, which is also sung between the verses as indicated above.

2. Arrange partners in a large single circle in an open space area and walk through the steps from the beginning to the end.

3. As soon as students grasp the sequence of steps, have them perform the dance with the music, which may be played on the piano, a tape, or simply sung by the students.

III–29   JINGLE BELLS   Grades 2–6

A double circle formation with partners is needed to dance on the chorus only.

Objective: To participate in an organized dance in a rhythmic fashion.

Formation: Partners form a double circle with boys in the inner circle and girls in the outer circle in a large open space area. Partners face each other for this dance.

Jingle Bells

James Pierpont

Dance Steps:

Partners form a double circle with boys on the inside and girls on the outside. Partners face each other.

Measure 1:   Slap knees three times to the rhythm of "Jingle Bells."

Measure 2:	Clap hands three times to the rhythm of "Jingle Bells."
Measures 3–4:	Partners hook right elbows and swing around.
Measures 5–6:	Take four fast step-slides in a counterclockwise direction (to the boy's left and the girl's right). Each step-slide must take one beat. Partners hold both hands.
Measures 7–8:	Take four fast step-slides in the opposite direction (clockwise direction)
Measures 9–12:	Repeat the steps given in measures 1–4.
Measures 13–14:	Partners hold hands in a promenade position and walk forward (counterclockwise direction) four steps (two steps to a beat).
Measures 15–16:	Boys stand still while girls move forward to a new partner to repeat the entire dance.

Procedure:

1. Review "Jingle Bells" by having them sing it once or twice.
2. Arrange partners in a double circle with boys on the inside and girls on the outside. The dance begins with partners facing each other. Go through the movements without singing the song, though words may be said at the appropriate time. Probably the most difficult part occurs in measures 5–8 with four fast sliding steps in one direction and then four in the other.
3. After the group is able to walk through the steps reasonably well, perform the dance with the music, which may be sung by the group or played by a pianist.

III–30   THE BEAR WENT OVER THE MOUNTAIN   Grades 3–6

This is a simple folk dance, somewhat reminiscent of the square dance. A reel formation is used.

Objective: To participate in an organized dance in a rhythmic fashion.

Formation: Two lines facing each other, with partners in opposite lines in an open space area are required. Each reel (pair of lines) should consist of eight to sixteen people.

The Bear Went Over the Mountain

Oh, the bear went o - ver the moun - tain, The bear went o - ver the moun - tain, The bear went o - ver the moun - tain To see what he could

see.___ And all that he could see, ___ And all that he could see, ___ Was the oth - er side of the moun - tain, The oth - er side of the moun - tain, The

oth - er side of the moun - tain Was all that he could see.___

Dance Steps:

Partners form two long lines, facing each other, with boys in one line and girls in the other. There may be from four to eight people in each line. The lines should be separated by about eight to twelve feet.

Measures 1–4:   Partners walk forward (toward each other) and bow or curtsy. They then walk backward into place and bow or curtsy again.

Measures 5–8:   The two lines walk toward each other and girls walk under the boys' raised, joined hands. As soon as the lines have completed the exchange of sides, they turn around and face each other.

Measures 9–10:   Clap three times and hold.

Measures 11–12: Clap three times and hold.

Measures 13–16: Hook right elbows with partner in opposite line and swing around.

Measures 17–20: Hook left elbows and swing around with partner, ending on opposite sides.

The group should repeat the entire dance one more time in order for the girls to raise their joined hands for the boys to go underneath.

Procedure:

1. Teach or review the above song.
2. Walk through the steps for the first eight measures (walking forward, bowing, walking backward, bowing). Do this much with the music.
3. Go through the clapping for measures 8–12. The students should clap on each of these words in this section: *all, he, see.* Sing these measures and clap as described.
4. Go through measures 1–12 with the music.
5. Walk through the steps for measures 13–20. As soon as they are ready, do this last section with the music, as they sing.
6. Do the entire dance with the music, including the second time through where the opposite line goes under the raised hands of the girls.

III–31   MAMA SENT ME TO THE SPRING   Grades 2–6

Squares of four children each are formed and they do a series of simple movements.

Objective: To participate in an organized folk dance in a rhythmic fashion.

Formation: Arrange partners in small squares of four people each in an open space area. One set of partners faces the other set of partners initially. During the chorus, partners will face each other.

Mama Sent Me to the Spring

Verse 2:

First he gave a peach to me,
Then he gave a pear.
But I said I must go home,
Could not linger there.
Chorus:

Me-o my, my, my, Me-o my.
Me-o my, my, my, Me-o my.

Verse 3:

So I gave him back his peach,
Gave him back his pear.
Ran home from the silver spring,
Left him standing there.
Chorus:

Me-o my, my, my, Me-o my.
Me-o my, my, my, Me-o my.

Dance Steps:

Two sets of partners form a square with the girl of one partner set facing the girl of the other partner set, and the boys facing each other. The two partner sets should be approximately eight feet apart.

Verse 1:

Measures 1–4:   The boy and girl in opposite corners of the square walk to the center, bow, and walk backward to place.

Measures 5–8: The opposite boy and girl repeat the action outlined in measures 1–4.

Chorus:

Measure 9: Partners quickly turn to face each other and tap both hands with their partner's hands twice (on the beat).

Measure 10: Each person slaps the upper legs three times to the rhythm of *My, my, my.*

Measure 11: Tap the partner's hands twice as in measure 9.

Measure 12: Slap the upper legs once on *my* and hold two beats.

Measures 13–15: Repeat actions in measures 9–11.

Measure 16: Turn around and face the other partner set ready to sing verse 2 (or 3).

Verses 2 and 3:

Measures 1–4: Boy and girl in opposite corners of the square skip to the center, hook right elbows, swing around, and return to place.

Measures 5–8: Opposite boy and girl repeat the action outlined in measures 1–4.

Chorus:

Measures 9–16: Repeat all actions outlined for Verse 1.

Procedure:

1. Teach or review above song, singing all three verses.
2. Pair off children and do motions of the chorus without the music at first. As soon as they seem ready, do the motions with the music (as they sing or the piano is played).
3. Organize partners in squares of four. Partners should stand side by side facing the person of the same sex in the opposite partner set (girls face each other as do boys). Walk through the outlined movements of the entire dance (all three verses with the chorus after each verse). When they are ready, do the dance with the music.

III–32   WHO HAS THE DIME?   Grades 3–6

A leader slips a dime (or other small object) into the hand of one person in the circle. The dime is then passed furtively from one person to another, and the leader must guess who has it at the end of the song.

Objective: To attempt to pass a dime or other object from person to person during the song without letting the leader know where it is.

Formation: The entire group forms a single circle in an open space area. One person from the circle is selected to stand in the middle and be the leader.

Who Has the Dime?

Harriet Reeves

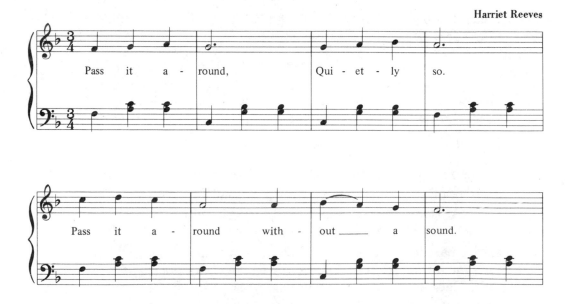

Tell me, Joan, tell me, Joe,

Who has the dime, who has it this time.

Game:

All students stand in a single circle with their left hands extended, except for one student who stands in the center. This student, called the leader, hands a dime or other object to someone in the circle who will begin passing it with his right hand. As the song begins all students in the circle touch the left hand of the person on the left (as the left hands are extended for touching, right hands are used to do the touching) three times (on each beat of measure one); each person in the circle will then touch his own hand three times (measure two) with his right hand; each will then touch the left hand of the person on the right three times (measure three). To complete the cycle, each will then touch his own left hand three times (measure 4). The game continues in this fashion as students pass the dime from one person to another until the end of the song. At this point, the leader tries to guess who has the dime. If he guesses correctly, the person who had the object takes the place of the leader in the center of the circle, and the old leader becomes a part of the circle.

The circle students should try to fool the leader by pretending to pass the dime at times.

Procedure:

1. Teach the above song.

2. Students form a circle and all extend their left hands which are almost closed (to hide the fact that they do or do not have the dime). Give one student a dime in his right hand and ask him to start passing it as he taps three times each (on the beat) the left hands of the following people in succession and without missing a beat:

    A. The left hand of the person on the left side.
    B. His own left hand.
    C. The left hand of the person on the right side.
    D. His own left hand.

    As soon as the above cycle is completed, it is repeated three more times.

3. As soon as students are able to follow the procedure fairly well without the passing of the dime becoming obvious, play the game as they sing the song. At the end of each verse, the leader, or the student in the center, states who he thinks has the dime. If he is correct, the two students exchange places and the game resumes with the new leader.

III–33　　FOUR IN A BOAT　　　　　　Grades 3–6

This is a circle game with four people in the center who choose partners from the outer circle.

Objective:　To play the game in a rhythmic fashion.

Formation:　The game begins with four children standing in the center of a circle made by the remaining children.

Four in a Boat

Appalachian Singing Game

1. Four in a boat and the tide rolls high,
Four in a boat and the tide rolls high,
Four in a boat and the tide rolls high,
Wait-ing for a pret-ty one to come by'n by.

Verse 2:

Choose your partner and stay all day,
Choose your partner and stay all day,
Choose your partner and stay all day,
We don't care what the old folks say.

Verse 3:

Eight in a boat and it won't go 'round,
Eight in a boat and it won't go 'round,
Eight in a boat and it won't go 'round,
Swing that pretty one you've just found.

Game:

Verse 1: Four children in the center swing their arms high to the center and back to their sides as the outside circle skips in a counterclockwise direction.

Verse 2: The outside circle stands clapping as each child in the center selects a partner to join him in the center. The eight in the center form a circle.

Verse 3: The outside circle skips in a counterclockwise direction as the eight in the center circle slide laboriously in the opposite direction. On the last phrase, the four inside couples swing partners with hooked right elbows. The game continues with the four newly chosen students remaining in the center of the circle, and the other four joining the outer circle.

Procedure:

1. Teach the above song, singing all three verses.

2. Select four students to go in the center of the circle and ask all others to form the outer circle. Walk through the movements associated with each verse as outlined above.

3. As soon as children demonstrate their understanding of the game in step 2, play the game as they sing the song. The series of three verses may be repeated as often as you wish.

III–34   MINUET   Grades 3–6

This well-known minuet consists of simple, but dignified, movements performed in a slow tempo.

Objective: To participate in an organized dance in a rhythmic manner.

Formation: Partners compose a double circle, facing counterclockwise, in an open space area. The boys will be in the inner circle and the girls in the outer circle next to their partners.

Minuet

Beethoven

Dance Steps:

Partners are arranged in a double circle with the boys in the inner circle and the girls in the outer circle. The partners face counter-clockwise, holding their joined inner hands aloft.

PART A

Measure 1:	Starting with inside feet (right feet for boys and left feet for girls), partners take three steps forward (one step per beat).
Measure 2:	Point outside toes (left toes for boys and right toes for girls) and hold in that position for two beats. On the third beat, step once with the outside feet.
Measure 3:	Point inside toes and hold for two beats. On the third beat, step once on the inside feet.
Measure 4:	Point outside toes and hold for three beats.
Measure 5:	Same as measure one except using opposite feet.
Measure 6:	Same as measure two except using opposite feet.
Measure 7:	Partners drop hands and turn in a circle away from their partners (three steps on the beat).
Measure 8:	Partners take one additional step to face their partners and then bow or curtsy.

Repeat of Measures 1–8: Repeat all steps exactly as outlined above.

PART B

Measure 1:	Partners quickly join right hands and hold them aloft and step three times starting with inside feet.
Measure 2:	Point outside toes and hold position for three beats.
Measure 3:	Take three steps starting with outside feet.
Measure 4:	Point inside toes and hold position for three beats. Partners should be facing in the same direction as they were at the beginning of Part B.

Measures 5–8: Same as measures 1–4 for Part B.

Repeat of Measures 1–7: Same as above.

Repeat of Measure 8: Take one step and bow or curtsy.

Procedure:

1. As this dance is slower and more dignified than many folk dances, it may be important to give students a little background to whet their appetites for learning it. When it was first brought to Paris, France, from outlying areas, it was a lively dance. As the nobility during the reigns of Louis XIV and XV began to use the dance extensively at their parties, it was slowed down and performed in a dignified and courtly manner to accommodate their formal dress, huge skirts, and high upswept hair styles. Pointing their toes enabled the ladies to show their pointed slippers and small feet and the gentlemen to show their silk stockings and buckled shoes.

2. Arrange the partners in a double circle around a large open space area. Walk through the steps for Part A. It is important that the steps are executed on certain beats as indicated in the music above. As soon as the group is able to do the steps in sequence for Part A, have them perform it with the music.

3. Walk through the steps for Part B. Call attention to the new position (partners are now holding right hands and are facing in opposite directions). When they can walk through the steps, perform it with the music.

4. Perform both parts with the music without pause if possible. (It may take several days of practice for students to do the steps without errors.) As they refine the dance, help them in the graceful execution of the steps and in learning to step with pointed toes.

III–35   LA RASPA—Mexican Folk Dance   Grades 3–6

A Mexican folk dance that features hopping from one foot to the other in the first half and doing a fast waltz step on the second half.

Objective: To move in rhythm through a sequence of dance steps.

Formation: All those participating in the dance will form two straight lines facing each other in an open space area.

La Raspa

Mexican Folk Dance

Hop right, hop left, hop right, Hop left, then right,

then left, Hop right, hop left, hop right. Then left, then right, then

Fast Waltz Step

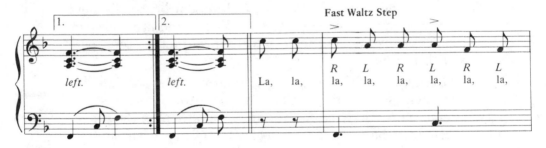

1. left. 2. left. La, la, la, la, la, la, la, la,
R L R L R L

R L R L R L etc.
la, la. etc.

Procedure:

1. It may be helpful for students to sing through the song using the descriptive words on the first part and the *las* on the second part.

2. Before asking students to come to the open space area, rehearse the two basic steps used in the dance. The first step consists of extending the right heel out in front as you hop; then extending the left heel out with a hop; and then the right heel again. This alternate extension of the heels three times with a slight pause afterward occurs three more times. See the words to the first half for hopping cues.

   The second step that needs to be rehearsed is the waltz step. The basic waltz step is:

   A. Step forward with the right foot; step forward with the left foot; bring the right foot beside the left foot.

   B. Step forward with the left foot; step forward with the right foot (the two feet will be apart); bring the left foot beside the right foot.

   The two steps above are repeated over and over, going in whatever direction is required (forward, backward). The waltz step should be practiced until students feel comfortable with it as it will be done rather rapidly in the dance.

3. Boys should line up in one straight line (four to eight) and girls in another straight line facing the boys. A hat (or other object) should be placed between each boy and girl facing each other. (If there are six couples, six hats will be needed). Children place their hands on their hips and do the first step of extending alternate heels as they hop.

4. On the second part, girls place both hands behind their backs and do the waltz step around the hats as the boys clap on the accents (if they have a problem with the waltz step, they could make up their own step).

5. Repeat the entire song, everyone extending alternate heels with a hop, as in step 3, on the first part.

6. On the second part, boys place both hands behind their backs and do the waltz step around the hats as the girls clap on the accents.

7. Repeat the entire song a third time, doing the same movement on the first half. On the second half, both the boys and girls do the waltz step around the hats, with right hands joined and raised over the hats and moving in a counterclockwise direction.

8. If the waltz step in the second half of the dance proves to be too difficult, this alternate step may suffice: partners hook right elbows and skip or swing around without the hat in the center.

III–36   SACRAMENTO   Grades 3–6

Squares of eight students each do a series of square dance steps, such as honoring partners and corner, and do-si-do.

Objective: To do a series of steps in a rhythmic manner.

Formation: Four couples form a square or quadrille in an open space area. There can be as many squares or quadrilles as desired.

Sacramento

To the tune of "The Camptown Races" by Stephen Foster

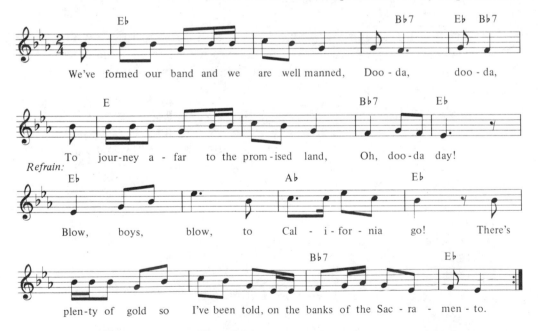

Formation: Four couples in a square with the couples numbered one, two, three, and four. Couples one and three face, and couples two and four face.

Dance Steps:

Measures 1-2:   The boy of couple one and the girl of couple three come to the center of the square, bow or curtsy, and return to place.

Measures 3-4:   The boy of couple three and the girl of couple one come to the center of the square, bow or curtsy, and return to place.

Measures 5-6:   The boy of couple two and the girl of couple four come to the center, bow or curtsy, and return.

Measures 7-8:   The boy of couple four and the girl of couple two come to the center, bow or curtsy, and return.

Measures 9-12:   All couples hook right elbows and swing.

Measures 13-16: All couples hook left elbows and swing.

(Repeat of song)

Measures 1-2:   Boy of one and girl of three do-si-do.

Measures 3-4:   Boy of three and girl of one do-si-do.

Measures 5-6:   Boy of two and girl of four do-si-do.

Measures 7-8:   Boy of four and girl of two do-si-do.

Measures 9-16:   Same as above.

Procedure:

1. While it is not necessary, you might have students sing the song.
2. Review square dance terminology that is used in this dance.
3. Call eight persons (four couples) to the front and walk them through the steps of the dance as outlined above.
4. Do the dance as the group sings the song or someone plays it. Call up as many people as the open space area can hold to form squares to do the dance. It may be wise to walk the new people through the steps before doing the dance with the music.

III–37   CHEBOGAH (THE BEETLE)   Grades 3–6

A circular formation is used in this Hungarian folk dance, which features a step-together movement.

Objective: To perform a series of dance movements in a rhythmic fashion.

Formation: Partners form a circle in a large open space area.

Chebogah (The Beetle)

Hungarian Folk Dance

In a cir-cle slide to left and don't be slow,
For-ward with a walk-ing step, then back in place,

To the right we slide a-gain as back we go.
Skip with el-bows joined and then your part-ner face.

Side-ward glide, side-ward glide, to the cen-ter glide,
Fast-er now, fast-er now, fast-er in and out,

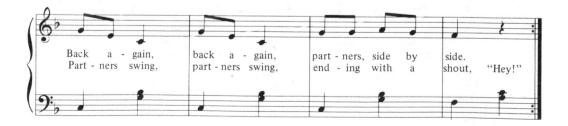

Back a-gain, back a-gain, part-ners, side by side.
Part-ners swing, part-ners swing, end-ing with a shout, "Hey!"

Formation: Partners form a large circle in an open space area.

Dance Steps:

> Measures 1–4:   Do four step-togethers to the right (one step-together per measure).
>
> Measures 5–8:   Do four step-togethers to the left.
>
> Measures 1–4 (Repeat): Take four steps into the center of the circle and four steps back out (one step per beat).
>
> Measures 5–8 (Repeat): Drop hands and hook right elbows with partner and swing around. On measure 8, face partner and hold both of partner's hands. The partners' sides should be toward the center of the circle ready for the next step.
>
> Measures 9–12:   Each set of partners takes four step-togethers toward the center of the circle.
>
> Measures 13–16: Take four step-togethers back to prior position.
>
> Measures 9–10 (Repeat): Take two step-togethers toward center of circle.
>
> Measures 11–12 (Repeat): Take two step-togethers back out.
>
> Measures 13–16 (Repeat): Partners hook right elbows and swing around. On the second beat of measure 16, everyone raises the left arm (with closed hand to make a fist) and shouts "Hey!"

Procedure:

1. Teach the above song if desired. If there is no one to play the piano, students may furnish their own music by singing.

2. Demonstrate the steps by calling up four couples to form a circle in the open space area. These four couples should join hands when they form the circle. Walk through the steps for measures one through eight plus the repeat of those measures. The step-together movement is the basic step used throughout the entire dance and consists simply of moving one foot out to the side and sliding the other foot next to it. When the group performs the steps for the first half of the dance well enough, have them do it with the music.

3. Walk through the steps for measures nine through sixteen and the repeat of those measures. Put the steps to the music when the group is ready.

4. Do the entire dance with the music.

5. Call up the remainder of the group, or as many as there is room for in the open space area. Walk through the steps with the new people and then do the entire dance with the music.

III-38   SCOTTISH DANCE   Grades 3-6

This Scottish folk dance uses a schottische step, plus others.

Objective: To perform a series of dance steps in rhythm to the music.

Formation: Partners form a single circle in an open space area.

Scottish Dance

Scottish Folk Tune

Formation: Partners form a single circle and face each other. The left arm should be raised over the head and the right hand on the hip.

Dance Steps:

Measure 1:	Point the right toe to the side while hopping on the left foot (one beat); bring the right foot behind the left knee while hopping on the left foot (one beat); Point the right toe out to the side again while hopping on the left foot (one beat); bring the right foot in front of the left knee while hopping on the left foot (one beat).
Measure 2:	Do one schottische step to the right—move the right foot to the side, slide the left foot beside the right, take another step to the right side with the right foot, and hop on the right foot.
Measure 3:	This is the same step as in measure one, but with the left foot. Point the left toe to the side while hopping on the right foot (one beat); bring the left foot behind the right knee while hopping on the right foot (one beat); point the left toe out to the side again while hopping on the right foot (one beat); bring the left foot in front of the right knee while hopping on the left foot (one beat).
Measure 4:	Do one schottische step to the left—move the left foot to the side, slide the right foot beside the left, take another step to the left side with the left foot, and hop on the left foot.
Measure 5:	Partners hook right arms and place left hands on their hips. They do a schottische step (step, step, step, hop) as they move around in a small circle.
Measures 6, 7:	Continue to do two more schottische steps.
Measure 8:	Boys move forward (counterclockwise) to meet a new partner as girls move backward (clockwise) to meet a new partner. Repeat the entire dance.

Procedure:

1. After introducing the dance, teach the basic steps used in the dance—the step described in measures one and three and the schottische step. See above directions for a description of the steps.

2. Walk through the sequence of steps in measures one through four. After they are able to do the steps smoothly, put these steps to the music, which may be played on the piano or on a tape recorder. (If the music is taped, it should be played approximately four to eight times in its entirety.)

3. Walk through the steps in measures five through eight. After the students are able to do the steps smoothly, put these steps to the music.

4. Do the entire dance with the music several times. It is suggested that six to eight couples be placed in each large circle and that the music be repeated on the tape the same number of times as there are couples in each circle. This way, each person in the circle will be partners with all others of the opposite sex in the circle during the entire dance.

III–39   THE VIRGINIA REEL   Grades 4–6

This is the traditional square dance often done by pioneer families moving westward in the early years of our country.

Objective: To perform a series of square dance steps in a rhythmic fashion.

Formation: Students form two straight lines of six each with partners in opposite lines facing each other. A large open space area is required. As many reels as space allows may be formed.

Music: A number of songs would be appropriate for use with these steps. Recordings are available from KIMBO Educational, P.O. Box 477, Long Branch, N.J. 07740.

In case no recordings or music are available, the music to "Oh! Susanna" by Stephen C. Foster is included here.

Oh! Susanna

Words and Music by
Stephen C. Foster

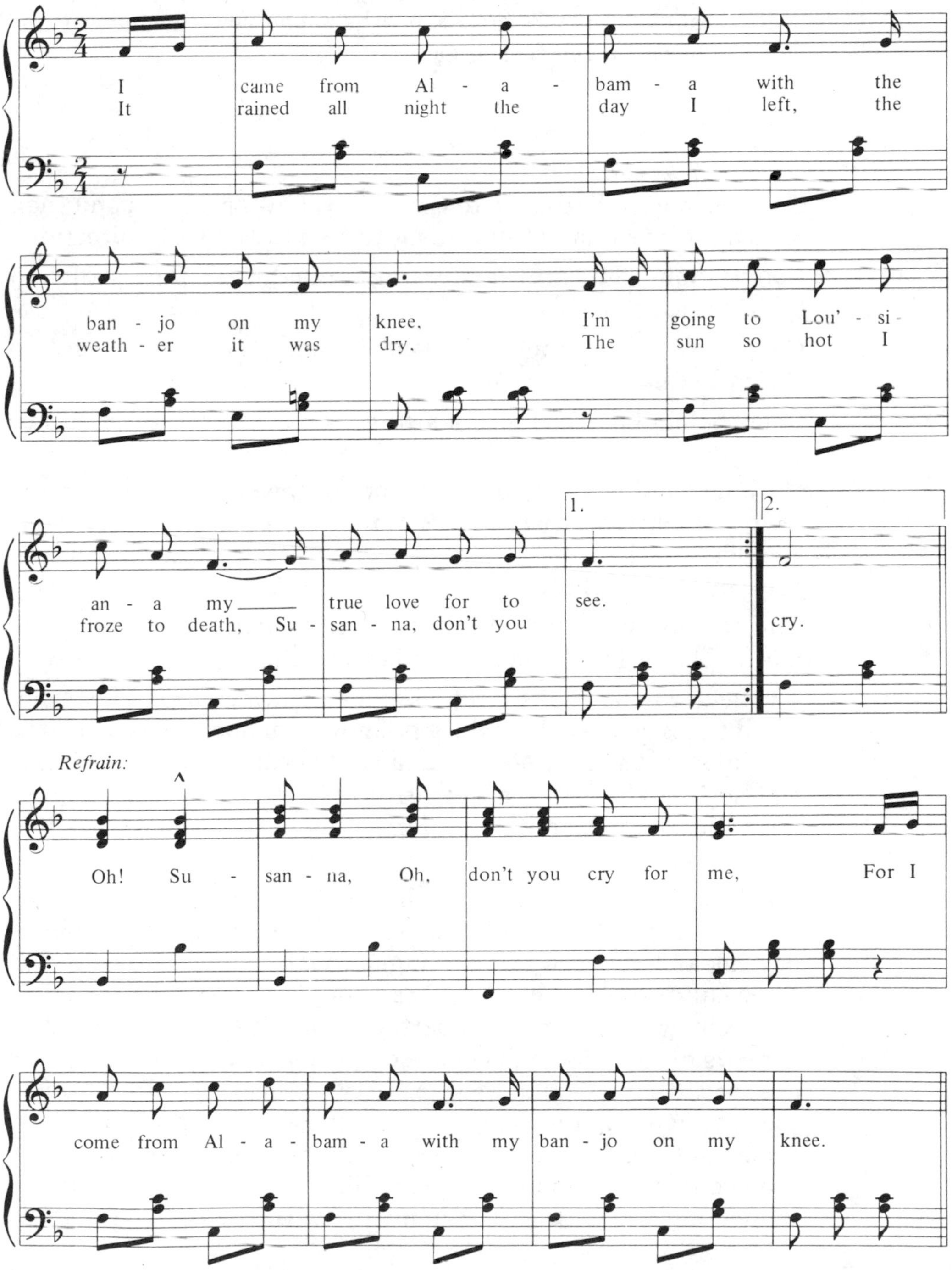

Formation: Reel formation is required for this dance. Students form two straight lines of six people each, with partners in opposite lines facing each other. The two lines should be eight to ten feet apart.

Dance Steps:

1. Couples in each line come to the center, bow or curtsy, and then return to their places (continuing to face in the same direction).

2. Couples join right arms and swing around; then they return to their places.

3. Couples join left arms and swing around; then they return to their places.

4. Couples join both hands and swing around; then they return to their places.

5. Each person folds both arms in front of the chest and does a do-si-do with his partner (partners pass right shoulder to right shoulder, back to back, and left shoulder to left shoulder and back into original places).

6. The head couple joins both hands and sashays sideward to the foot of the reel and back to the head again.

7. The head couple hooks right elbows and swings around one and a half times so that the girl's left elbow is in position to hook the left elbow of the first boy remaining at the head of the boy's line and so that the boy's left elbow (head couple) is in position to hook the left elbow of the girl remaining at the head of the girl's line.

8. The head couple should do an allemande left and right down the entire reel to the foot. Allemande left and right: the head couple boy hooks left elbows and swings around once with the girl at the head of the reel line; the head couple boy then extends his right elbow and swings his partner in the middle once; he then extends his left elbow to hook the left elbow of the second girl in the reel: after swinging once, he extends his right elbow to join that of his partner and swings around once. This procedure continues until he has swung every girl in the reel. Meanwhile, the head couple girl is doing the same thing with the boys, alternately meeting her partner in the middle with the right elbow and swinging.

9. After finishing the allemande left and right, ending by swinging the partner in the middle, the head couple will join both hands and sashay sideways to the head of the reel (the boy should be on the boys' side of the reel and the girl on the girls' side). At the head of the reel, the head couple casts off—the boy goes behind the boys' line with all the boys in order following him, and the girl goes behind the girls' line with all the girls in order following her.

10. The head couple meets at the foot of the reel and forms an upraised arch with their hands. All the other couples meet their partners and join both hands as they go through the arch formed by the head couple and form two straight lines. The old head couple is at the foot and a new head couple at the head of the reel ready to go through the sequence of dance steps all over again. This repetition is continued until all couples in the reel have been the head couple.

Procedure:

1. Form a reel consisting of two lines with six people in each line facing each other. Boys should be in one line and girls in the other, with partners facing each other. Walk through steps one through five. When the group feels comfortable with this much, do the steps to the music.

2. Walk through steps six through ten. The allemande left and right may take a little extra work. After the group feels comfortable with these steps, do the steps to the music.

3. Do the entire dance with the music. The dance should be repeated until all couples in the reel have danced the part of the head couple.

III–40   THE BUNNY HOP   Grades 4–6

This popular party activity requires participants to form a long straight line and contains a few simple hopping steps, that are done over and over again.

Objective: To perform a series of steps in rhythm to the music.

Formation: Students form a long straight line with their hands on the shoulders of the person in front and move around a large open space area.

Music: A recording of "The Bunny Hop" may be bought in any music store that sells "Golden Oldies," or ordered from a school supply business that handles school recordings.

Procedure:

1. Before forming the long line to do the dance, have the students practice the dance steps in front of their desks.

2. Demonstrate the following steps:

   a. Hop on the left foot while the right heel is extended at about a 45-degree angle between the front and side. Hop on the left foot again when you bring the right foot back in place beside the left foot. These hops are done on the beat. Do this step twice.

   b. Hop on the right foot as you extend the left heel at about a 45-degree angle between the front and side. Hop on the right foot again as you bring the left foot back in place beside the right foot. Do this step twice.

   c. Make a big hop forward (two beats), a big hop backward (two beats), and three small hops forward (one hop per beat). All these hops are to be done with both feet together as a bunny would hop.

   A recap of the above steps with the beats follows:

   / 1   2   3   4/   / 1   2   3   4 /
   R Heel out, in, out, in;   L Heel out, in, out, in

   /   1   2   3   4/ 1   2   3   4 /
   Big hop front,   Big hop back; Hop, hop, hop, rest.

This same step sequence is done over and over again until the end of the record (or until the students are exhausted).

3. Invite students to try the dance steps. As soon as they are able to do them without the music, put them to the music.

4. Ask students to form a long line with each student's hands placed on the shoulders of the student in front and do the steps around the room in a large open space area.

III–41   ALLEY CAT   Grades 4–6

A simple sequence of steps that can be learned quickly. No special formation is required. No partners are needed.

Objective: To perform a series of dance steps in rhythm to the music.

Formation: No special formation is required, but students need room to move unobstructed. If you wish, they may all stand in straight lines in an open space area, facing in the same direction.

Music: A recording of "Alley Cat" may be bought in any music store that sells "Golden Oldies," or ordered from a school supply company that sells recordings.

Procedure:

1. Ask students to stand in straight lines in an open space area, or beside their desks, to perform the dance "Alley Cat."

2. Demonstrate the following steps:

   a. Begin with feet together in a standing position. Move the right foot out to the right and back in again (one beat each movement). This is done twice.

   b. Move the left foot out to the left and back in again (one beat each movement). Do this twice.

   c. Move the right foot backward and then together (twice).

   d. Move the left foot backward and then together (twice).

   e. Raise the right knee and lower it back to the original stance (twice).

 f. Raise the left knee, and then lower it (twice).

 g. Raise the right knee and lower it again (once).

 h. Raise the left knee and lower it again (once).

 i. Everyone claps and rests one beat, then turns to the right with a jump (90-degree turn). If the students were originally facing north, they would now be facing east. These movements occur over four beats.

A recap of the steps above with the beats follows:

```
 / 1     2     3    4 /     1     2     3     4 /
RF side, back, side, back;  LF side, back, side, back;
 / 1     2          3      4 /
RF back, together, back, together;
 / 1     2          3      4 /
LF back, together, back, together
 /1     2    3    4 /     1     2     3     4 /
RK up, down, up, down   LK up, down, up, down;
 / 1     2           3    4 /     1     2     3    4 /
RK up, down;  LK up, down;   Clap and turn (rest).
```

 j. The entire step sequence starts all over again.

The sequence of steps is repeated at least four times, or until the pupils are facing in their original directions, or until the music ends. The pupils always turn to the right on the last phrase (clap and turn).

 3. After a demonstration of the steps, and a walk-through by the students, try the dance with the music. At first, it may be helpful to call out the steps as they occur.

III–42 WEGGIS   Grades 4–6

A Swiss dance featuring the schottische step that can be challenging to upper elementary students.

Objective: To perform a series of dance steps in rhythm to the music.

Formation: Partners form a double circle in a large open space area.

Weggis

Swiss Folk Song

From Lu - cerne to __ Weg - gis on,
Shoes or stock - ings __ we won't don,
Hol - di - ri - di - a,

Hol - di - ri - a, Hol - di - a.
Hol - di - ri - di - a,

Hol - di - ri - dir - a, Hol - di - ri - a.
Hol - di - a.

Formation: Partners form a double circle facing in a counterclockwise direction. The girl stands at the boy's right with
her left hand on his right shoulder and his right hand
around her waist.

Dance Steps:

Measures 1–4:   Take four schottische steps (step, step, step,
hop) forward, starting on outside feet. Each
schottische step takes four beats.

Measures 1–4 (Repeat): Take four schottische steps backward.

Measures 5-6:   Each partner takes one schottische step diagonally away from the partner during measure 5, turns diagonally toward the partner and takes another schottische step during measure 6. This should bring the partners back together.

Measures 7-8:   Partners face, join right hands in an upraised position, and do four step-hops around each other so that they return to their position at the end of measure 4.

Measures 5-8 (Repeat): Same steps as in measures 5-8 above.

Procedure:

1. Teach the above song.

2. Demonstrate the two basic steps used in the dance and have students practice them in front of their desks. The two steps are as follows:

   a. Step, step, step, hop: If they start on the right foot, then they step right, left, right, and then hop on the right foot. The next step will begin on the left foot: step left, right, left, and hop on left foot.

   b. Step, hop: If this step begins on the right foot, then they step on the right, and hop on the right; the next step begins on the left, and they hop on the left foot.

3. Arrange partners in a double circle with girls on the boys' right and facing in a counterclockwise direction. Walk through the steps for the first eight measures and then do the steps with the music as soon as the students are ready.

4. Walk through the steps for the last eight measures. Special attention may need to be paid to the one schottische step diagonally away from the partner and then another schottische step diagonally back toward the partner. Do the steps with the music as soon as the students are ready.

5. Perform the entire dance with the music.

III–43   THE HORA (Israeli Folk Dance)   Grades 4–6

This is an Israeli circle game often done at Jewish gatherings. It contains a few basic steps which are repeated over and over.

Objective: To perform a series of movements in rhythm to the music.

Formation: All participants form a circle in a large open space area.
Their hands should be joined.

Havah Nagila

Israeli Folk Dance

Formation: All participants form a circle and place their extended hands on each other's shoulders.

Dance Steps:

This folk dance consists of six steps (one step per beat), which are repeated over and over throughout the dance.

Step one: Begin with feet side by side. Step to the side with the right foot.

Step two: Put the left foot behind the right foot and place your weight on it.

Step three: Step to the right on the right foot and place your weight on it.

Step four: Kick the left foot across the front of the right foot while hopping on the right foot at the same time.

Step five: Step down on the left foot (remember the left foot is in front of the right foot and perhaps across it in front where you just kicked it in step four). Place your weight on the left foot.

Step six: Kick the right foot out to the front while hopping on the left foot at the same time.

Continue to repeat all six steps through the music.

Procedure:

1. Demonstrate the Hora. Outline the above steps and walk the students through them.

2. When students are able to walk through the steps fairly well, add the music.

3. All participants should then form a circle, placing their hands on each other's shoulders. Do the dance as outlined above.

Index

Note: Italicized entries are music titles.

Academic Skills Index

239

Subject Index

ANIMALS

CUMULATIVE SONGS

DANCES AND ACTIVITIES FROM DIFFERENT COUNTRIES

7   6/10/88